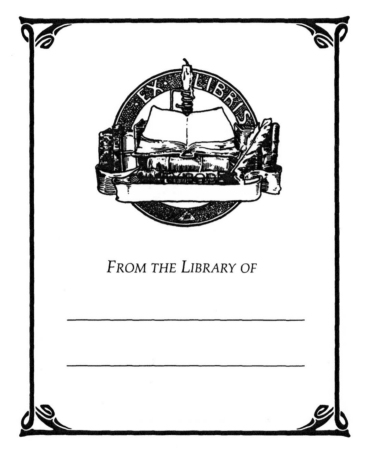

FROM THE LIBRARY OF

_____

_____

WHAT ARE YOU?

WHAT ARE YOU?

IMELDA OCTAVIA SHANKLIN

Unity Classic Library

unity®
HOUSE

Unity Village, Missouri

Second edition 2004; fifth printing 2007

What Are You? is a member of the
Unity Classic Library.

The Unity Classic Library is guided by the belief of Unity
cofounder Charles Fillmore that "whatever God has revealed to
man in one age He will continue to reveal to him in all ages."
The series projects Fillmore's vision of Unity as "a link in the
great educational movement inaugurated by Jesus Christ" to
help and teach humankind to use and prove eternal Truth.

To place an order, call the Customer Service Department at
1-800-669-0282 or go to *www.unityonline.org*. For information,
address Unity House, 1901 NW Blue Parkway, Unity Village,
MO 64065-0001.

First printing 1929 with twenty-one printings through 1995.
Second edition, 2004

Cover design by Gretchen West

Library of Congress Control Number: 2003114771
ISBN 0-87159-307-6
ISBN 978-0-87159-307-8
Canada BN 13252 9033 RT

"Spiritually, what are you? You are a soul that has forgotten its divine identity, a soul now struggling to remember, in the midst of time and in the confusions of experiences, that you are the living son of the living God."

Imelda Shanklin

CONTENTS

YOUR IDENTITY
Chapter 1

What are you? Until you can answer this question promptly and correctly at any time that it is asked, you do not know yourself well enough to trust yourself, to be happy, to be assured of continued safety and well-being.

I meet an intelligent-appearing, upstanding young man, and I ask him, "What are you?" He looks puzzled. I repeat the question. Then he smiles pleasantly, thinking that I have not correctly worded the query. He informs me, "I am Johnny Doe." To himself, he adds, "Twenty-two years of age, popular, law student, a man you will hear from later."

The answer that Johnny Doe gives me and the elaborations that he makes to himself do not respond to the question that I asked. He has not understood the question. He has translated it from the impersonal to the personal; his answer corresponds to his lack of understanding. He has answered the question, "Who are you?"

If you have been considering yourself wholly as a personal entity, you also will answer the question incorrectly when it is asked you. The error in your mind that causes you to assume the *who* when you should recognize the *what* is the source of every misunderstanding in life that perplexes you.

The chief misapprehension of the world concerning Jesus Christ has been that of considering Him from the personal side of life. Contemporaries,

5

ignorant of His greatest value, said of Him, "He is
the son of the carpenter"; "He is Moses or Elias."
Peter, unconfused by the personal, said to Him,
"Thou art the Christ, the Son of the living God."
The Christ placed His approval on this answer in the
significant words, "Blessed art thou . . . for flesh
and blood hath not revealed it unto thee, but my
Father who is in heaven."

The personal is the seen: body, conduct, situation.
The impersonal is the unseen: spirit, mind, revelation. Your intention translates the unseen into
the seen, and makes the *what* of life become the *who*
of life.

The personal, the *who*, can be changed. You
have changed it many times, and you will continue
to change it. This is not said to indicate reincar-
nation. It is said to indicate the changes that come
in body, conduct, and situation, in every life. These
changes make Baby Doe become Johnny Doe; they
make Johnny Doe grow successively into Lawyer
Doe, Judge Doe, Governor Doe. In all of Johnny
Doe's changes of relationship to the world, only
the *who* is concerned. The *what* is not affected. That
is changeless. It eternally will be what it eternally
has been. It is the divinity of which Peter said in
a moment of insight, "Thou art the . . . Son of the
living God."

In the fact that the personal can be changed lies
your hope of achievement. In the fact that the impersonal is changeless lies your assurance of an attainable perfection in the realms of conscious being.
From glory to glory passes the personal in its search

for the peace-bestowing impersonal, which has its home in the heart of God.

If discouragement assails you because of environment, tradition, or heredity, transfer your consideration from the personal to the impersonal. You are not characterless flesh and blood, unfavorable heredity, spineless nothingness. "Thou art the . . . Son of the living God." In your everlasting nature you are impersonal, impregnable. Square your consideration of life by these facts, and you will be supplied with ample courage for every demand.

When you identify yourself solely with the personal you are not satisfied. There is a lack for which you cannot account, but which is very real to you. If you should voice your feeling you perhaps would say, "I want something. I do not know what it is that I want, but when I receive what I want I shall be satisfied." Knowing the personal, only, you have but superficial knowledge of yourself. Beneath the surface the rich deeps of life summon you with overmastering appeal. Not knowing how to respond, you have a sense of confusion and restlessness.

So thin the screen between the personal and the impersonal, so transparent the floor that shuts the superficial from the deeps, your vision now and then is soothed by flashes of your divine identity, and you have momentary peace. But the flash passes, and again the night of nonrecognition closes about you.

Disquieting questions as to the why and the how of life cease when you begin to regard yourself as impersonal being manifesting as personality. You become immune to doubt when you learn that the impersonal is indestructible. Poise rules your life when you awaken to the fact that the changes which come to the personal are not the work of an agency outside yourself, but the registrations of your mental operations.

You know your starting point for a better manifestation when you see that in your present status of being you are triune. You can observe the three-sided aspect of your being by noticing the ways in which you think of yourself. The following points approximate your thoughts concerning your individuality:

First. You say, "I feel the assuring presence of a vast good, a something indefinable but infinitely desirable. It draws me toward itself with an irresistible sweetness." In this feeling you sense the eternal, changeless character of your being, which, in the language of religion, is called the spiritual you. As spiritual being you have identity with God, and because of identity you feel the presence of God as a vast good.

Second. You say, "I know. I think. I understand." These declarations are evidence that you have a mental character.

Third. You say, "my body"; "my circumstances"; "my life." These phrases show that you recognize a third state of being. This state is the physical you.

You must become acquainted with yourself in these three aspects of identity. You must distinguish between the three, that you may avoid confusion in the relations of cause and effect. You must remember that the three constitute you, and that you embrace all of them. When you have made these facts permanent in your mind you are properly equipped to begin the study of your identity.

What are you, spiritually?

If you accept some theological teachings on the subject, you will answer that you are a sinner, a lost soul. In so answering you speak in the consciousness of the personal, the changing. You cannot say that the impersonal, the changeless, sins or becomes lost. The impersonal is the spiritual; it is of God, and is identical with Him. If God can sin, so can the spiritual you, but not otherwise.

To become lost you must find a retreat outside of God. He occupies the universe. In any form of identity, there is no place where you can stray and be lost to Him, the Universal. If God can be lost, you can be lost, but under no other circumstances.

What theology calls a lost soul is a soul that has lost sight of God's omnipresence. In the personal you have acted ignorantly. The act of ignorance is the act of sin. In the impersonal you never have acted ignorantly, never have sinned. In the personal you have lost sight of God, but God never has lost sight of you. What is in the sight of God is not lost.

If you accept some metaphysical teachings you will answer the question by saying that you are divine perfection. The statement requires amplification, for it is true only of the impersonal. You must keep your terms accurate. The personal has not reached perfection. If it were perfect there would be no need of your trying to improve it; no need for so much as the affirmation of perfection. Body, conduct, situation, would conform to the absolute standard.

Of the personal, the answer of the theologian is perhaps true. Of the impersonal, the metaphysical answer is undeniably true. You mentally must distinguish as to which part of your nature you are describing. The personal can, and frequently does, act ignorantly—sinfully. The impersonal never can be ignorant, never can sin.

A man who is in a condition of amnesia does not remember his name, his home, his purposes. Temporarily, he is not conscious of his identity. His mind gropes in a fog of forgetfulness. There is a stage of his disorder in which hints, probings, do not help him. Mental oblivion has locked the man's consciousness upon itself. Spurred by the promptings of his submerged self, urged by the anxiety of eager friends, he struggles to remember who he is. Then some day comes a flicker, then comes a beam, and then the full light of recollection returns. The man has recovered consciousness of personal identity.

Spiritually, what are you?

You are a soul that has forgotten its divine identity, a soul now struggling to remember, in the midst of time and in the confusions of experiences, that you are the living son of the living God.

Spiritually, you are an idea in the mind of God. That idea must be given expression in you.

You are the son of God, but not always have you acted the part. If you will live in as full accordance with your divine nature as your present state of preparation makes possible, you will be made aware of your true identity. As the victim of amnesia persists in recalling personal identity, so you must persist in recalling spiritual identity. While you pray, read, meditate, practice spiritual Truth, a flicker, then a beam, then the full light of restored consciousness will dawn, and you will know yourself. In that knowing, the human estimate, in all that it values and in all that it decries, will be supplanted by the divine apprizement,

"Thou art my son;
This day have I begotten thee."

Mentally, what are you?

If your schooling has been meager, you may respond to this question by saying, "Ignorance. Everyone that I know is brighter than I; has had more opportunities than I; is better prepared to meet the world than I."

No matter what your educational training has been, you never will answer this question in the sentiment of the words quoted unless you speak of the personal. You may become intelligent, even if your schooling has been limited. To be intelligent is to be mentally fit to the degree of your intelligence. Schooling is an aid to intelligence, but lack of schooling does not condemn you to ignorance or to illiteracy. Books and methods of instruction are so numerous that you will become educated if you are sufficiently interested to do the work of educating yourself. Ignorance is found only in the personal, and the personal can be changed.

In declaring your mental identity do you say that you were a star student of some university? Do you rate yourself a philosopher, a poet, a "brainy man"? Do you say that you are wisdom?

If in the personal way you say, "I am ignorance," you may be stating a situation that exists. But if the situation does exist it need not continue to exist. The statement never is true of the impersonal, in which you are justified in saying, "I am wisdom." If you speak in wisdom, not often will you make the statement, "I am wisdom." You will discriminate sharply, to the end that the personal may not slip in and cause confusion. Exalted realizations of wisdom tend to check the use of the statement. The realizations suffice; words become pointless repetition. In the inner depths you know, "I am wisdom."

In your true mental identity you are the Mind of God. This Mind must be permitted to act in you. It knows all things; it makes no mistakes. In you it recognizes itself as beauty; in you it sustains its perfection. You become aware of its work in you when you do not crowd it aside by the arrogance of the personal mind.

Whence come the revelations that you receive? Why are you able to know anything? Revelation and knowledge come out of the Mind of God. That you have received is assurance that your receiving need not be stayed short of absoluteness.

If you put the Mind of God to uses that do not match the nature of God, you delay your mental growth. When you let the Mind of God act without interference on your part, you prosper in the work of regaining your mental identity. You abandon the habit of putting the Mind of God under the dictatorship of the personal mind. You enter the path of wisdom.

Physically, what are you?

If you believe that the personal is you, your answer to this question may be, "I am a wretched, deformed person; I have been physically unfit all my life." These statements can be true only of the personal, which you constantly are changing. The hurts and the limitations of the personal begin in the mental region. Thoughts of unfitness are defamation of character; they persuade your body to misrepresent your spiritual nature. Thoughts based on the recognition of your true identity will reconstruct your body in a way to make you physically fit. Your personal identity automatically adjusts itself to your thinking.

You may identify yourself with the physical in a statement to this effect, "I am a perfect physical specimen, one who always is physically fit." The perfections that you enumerate are possible; they are sure, if you subject the variable personal to the unvarying impersonal.

To build physical fitness where unfitness appears, more is required than mere wishing. Work is required, a regime of thought training that girds up the muscles of the mind and makes them alert, dependable. You must consciously connect with the Mind of God, and you must stay connected, that your body may be fed with His perfect life.

There is a mental operation that will do more for you than the act of ordinary thinking can do. It is the act of making your mind open toward the Mind of God; a making void the personal mind—a state of wonderment concerning the things that are in the

Mind of God. I know a woman who, quite unintentional of consequences, practiced the wondering method, and I know of the changes that the practice wrought in her body. The story is:

"I was studying the Sermon on the Mount. My attention was particularly challenged by the question, 'Which of you by taking thought can add one cubit unto his stature?' I worked on that question many weeks. I argued that Jesus did not mean to say that change could not be made; He was asking if any of His hearers had power sufficient to produce growth in the adult body. I said to myself that I supposed few persons would wish to add a whole cubit, but who was able to do it? I had no intention of producing a change in my body; I was interested in knowing the import of the question. A few weeks after I had dismissed this question and taken up another, I found that I had grown two inches in height. My dressmaker and the yardstick both attested the increase. Sympathetic friends acknowledged it; grudging friends admitted it. I was then ten years past the age at which bodily growth normally ceases."

In drawing distinctions between the personal and the impersonal, do not deny the fact of personality. Your personality reports the progress that you have made in the impersonal. It is the sum of all your former thinking. It is the monitor that keeps before your attention the necessity of doing better. It is the outside of the inside. It informs you, and you are encouraged or warned by its evidence. Denial discourages the body and ultimately dissolves it. Belief in the necessity of somatic death is denial of personality. Any denial of personality relaxes your grip on manifestation. Never think of personality as the source of life or as the transmitter of life. Never think of it as power, as influence, or as ideal. Remember that it is the observable form of your mental processes.

Physically you are the substance of God, molded in the matrix of your mind. If you are not satisfied with your personality you should remold it. For that purpose you have a mind.

The mental you is born of the spiritual you, and the physical you is your mind's outer translation of God's idea.

"Now are we children of God, and it is not yet made manifest what we shall be. We know that, if he shall be manifested, we shall be like him; for we shall see him even as he is." Let God manifest, and you will see that not only are you like Him, but that you are a form of Him.

Body, environment, and even associates are mental fingerprints by which your identity as a mental worker is established.

Your body is the blossom of your mind. Grief marks the face with lines that tell the story of mental suffering. If he who has grieved be baptized into a great joy, the grief lines are washed out and his face takes on the form and the glow of happiness. Mental habits cut deeper than facial lines betray. They mark the body and they influence organic functionings. Your body has a consciousness of its own; that consciousness is composed of what you have taught your body to believe and to demand.

Persons who think alike in important respects may suggest a resemblance not to be defined physically. I know two women who are said by their respective families to picture each other. The women are quite unlike in stature, coloring, featuring. But they are usually of one mind, especially in matters of religious or of moral import.

Family resemblances are produced by the like interests and the like tastes that usually are found in members of the same domestic group. It frequently is noted that as years pass there comes a resemblance between husband and wife which was not to be observed on their wedding day. Mental sympathies draw souls together, and like thinking produces like faces, like bodies. A chiropractor once said to me that the family back is as unmistakable as the family face. Effect is true to cause. What the eyes look upon is impressed on the flesh; the babe, looking into its mother's face, yields to the love curves of her expression, and grows into an image of its mother. I once heard a missionary tell of seeing two girls who had been rescued from a den of wolves in Asia. As babes they had been abandoned, and, in a measure duplicating the young lives of Romulus and Remus, had been mothered by a she-wolf. The children ran fleetly on all fours; they snarled and bit at their captors. The forehead retreated, the lower face protruded in unmistakable likeness to the foster-parent beast that had shown them more of mother love than their human mothers had shown.

What you look upon mentally or visually stamps your flesh with its likeness. Whatever of imperfection has been stamped upon your body can be removed therefrom by contemplation of the perfect. Untrue visioning, foolish thinking about life, cannot hurt the perfect life in you, but they weave a veil that to your eyes obscures the perfect and translates it into the flesh as imperfection. The man who suffers from amnesia does not recognize himself, but he is himself. You are the idea of God, capable of perfect translation. Some day you will become wholly awake to your divine identity, and will begin consciously to take on the image of perfection.

You never will know your true identity until you let the Mind of God instruct you as to what you are. When you become aware of your immortal nature, fear of death leaves you, and with it go all other forms of fear. All fear is based on fear of death. When you fear that your business may fail you say of it, "The thing is dying." When you fear that a friendship may terminate, you say, "It is dying out of my life." Consciousness of your true identity is awareness that you are as enduring as God. You cannot fear the thing that cannot take place. You know that God's immortality is your immortality, and that there can be no death.

Identity with God does not take away individuality; it enhances individuality, and gives you character superlative. It does not take away personality; it purifies and beautifies personality. It does not take away your joy of life; it refines your joy and increases it.

Perhaps you bewail a condition that you call repression. You say that circumstance or some person makes impossible your self-expression. In other words, you think that something extraneous to yourself has influence in your life greater than your influence; that the extraneous influence is malign, and that therefore you cannot mentally or physically do as well as you feel that you should do.

What do you wish to express? Whatever it may be, you will find your wish profited by your knowing what it is to express and how to express.

The word *express* means, "to set forth . . . to the observation or understanding." Previous to expression another act is performed. That act is impression. As used in this connection, the word *impress* means, "mark by pressure . . . To fix, as in the mind."

Your mind is impressed, is marked by the pressure of an idea, or you could have no impulse to express. Have you settled with yourself what it is that you wish to express? This you must do, to get sane action in the matter. If you say that you wish to express yourself you must choose which self you would give dominance in expression—the personal self or the impersonal self. Your genuine success will be fostered by putting the personal self under control of the impersonal self, and then proceeding with expression.

You cannot in an instant reverse the trend of your life as it has been set by your aims through aeons agone. When you begin to cultivate the liberating Mind of God, dreams, fantasies, impulses, which your mind infolds but of which you are not aware, surge forward. They, too, would express themselves. Therefore, take counsel with God; talk but little; boast not at all. Test your purpose and your meditated act by the rule of unity: If what you would do does not defy the integrity of the universe, you are safe in proceeding with expression. If what you would do falls short of the Golden Rule, abandon it. You have been expressing at variance with the universal good. That expression is the cause of your present distress. To improve conditions you must improve motives.

You express yourself all the time. If you have hypnotized yourself into a state of inertness by believing that agencies other than your own mind control your life, you express that conclusion. But you express.

To suppress means to put down or put an end to by force; to repress means to put back. If you believe that you can be suppressed or repressed, your belief sets forth to your own observation that someone is putting you down, putting you back. And you are right. Someone is putting the impersonal you down, putting the impersonal you back. That someone is the personal you. You are repressing and suppressing the best that is in you while you let its expression wait on the ignorance that makes you think that you are not supreme in your own life.

If you are repressed, suppressed, you are the represser, the suppresser. Persons and environment welcome all the good that you can give. Try expressing, freely, ungrudgingly, unsuspicious of ulterior purposes in others. You will find that you can express freedom and good in the very place where you have been expressing bondage to self-imposed inhibitions and to the resentments that have circled about you as birds of prey, incubated in your own mind. Thought and act are expression, whatever the thought, whatever the act.

You consciously contact the Mind of God through prayer. In conscious contact you receive. Prayer can take place at any time, in any environment. You do not have to go to a special place and shut yourself away from others, in order to reach God. If you feel that you must have a certain nook, a certain chair, a certain hour in which to approach God, you will not approach Him when you are denied these settings. You will duplicate the backslidings of the young woman who vindicated her fall from grace by saying, "How can you expect me to pray when Papa is too stingy to buy me a prayer rug?"

You do not have to go to any special place to think, and prayer is thinking toward God. If you wish to reserve a special place, set hours, and other features of formal prayer, there is no valid reason why you should not pray thus formally. But do not depend on special conditions. If, after your prayer is made, you leave God in the special place and shut Him out of your thoughts after the prayer period closes, your praying does not greatly benefit you. You will have to learn to contact Him in the open, and at all times. Spiritually you always are connected with Him. To pray, open your mind toward Him. Then, wherever you are, whatever the hour, you will receive according to your responsiveness to His ever-willing, ever-present power to bestow Himself.

Prayer is not in posture; it is not in a given form of phrases. Prayer is a relationship between you and God. That is, a relationship in which you consent to receive from God, who always is on the giving side.

You are God's manifest and manifesting idea.

Receiving God spiritually, you become aware of your spiritual identity:

I am an idea in the Mind of God. I let God's idea express in me.

Receiving God mentally, you become aware of your mental identity:

I am the Mind of God. I let the Mind of God inform me of my identity.

Receiving God physically, you become aware of your physical identity:

My body is the substance of God, manifesting in correspondence with His idea.

YOU ARE WHAT YOU THINK
Chapter 2

Your mind is your world.

Your thoughts are the tools with which you carve your life story on the substance of the universe. When you rule your mind, you rule your world. When you choose your thoughts, you choose results. The visible part of your life pours out of your mind, shaped and stamped by your thoughts, as surely as the coins of nations are shaped and stamped by the mechanisms used to convert ores into specie.

Mind is the source of feeling. You sometimes say: "I feel depressed. I feel as if something unpleasant were about to occur, but I do not know why I should feel so." The feeling of depression comes from your having subconsciously contacted something, which, if brought to the surface of consciousness, would cause you unhappiness.

You do not need to know what produces the disturbed condition of your mind, but you do need to know how to meet the condition. In an experience of this nature, you instantly should put yourself under special consecration to God and you should mentally release God in every realm of your mind. With all the force and all the clarity that you can summon, realize that you are an idea in the Mind of God. Not much argument will be required to convince you that an idea in the Mind of God always is safe, always is animated with the quality of being that we call joy. A conviction of these truths will dissipate forebodings.

A sense of being troubled may come through sympathetic union with one who is unhappy. Include others in your assurances of the protecting Presence. Your lasting individual good is enhanced by enhancement of the good of all. You are responsible for and responsible to everything that has existence in the realm of your abode. Train your mind to react sanely to the seethings of the human consciousness. Disorder exists for you while you acknowledge it. It ceases when you cease to support it by your acknowledgment. Do not let yourself be thrown into a panic by the feeling that something unpleasant may occur. Your feeling of impending danger is, in itself, danger. Your feeling of immanent safety is, in itself, safety. You experience what you think.

You sometimes say, "I feel glad about something, but I do not know what. I feel as if some great good is just around the corner, coming to meet me." You have this feeling because you have touched an unseen blessing; the feeling is trying to convey to your intelligence the fact that some particular good is ready for you. Or you may be sharing the good of another. When you have an experience of this nature, you should respond with deepest gratitude, for the experience is added evidence that you are regaining your identity of oneness with God. To accept the unseen good as real is to strengthen your mind in habits of correct thinking; is to give saner impulses to the human consciousness, from which you receive suggestions and to which you contribute suggestions.

Feeling is mental reaction to things recognized or unrecognized. In its earliest stage it is unformed thought. If you will watch your mental processes you will find that feeling precedes the definite thought. Your reaction to the thing unrecognized causes you to say that you feel that sorrow is near to you or that joy is near to you. As the feeling takes outline in definite thought, you know whether you are willing or unwilling to receive the thing that the thought specifies. From that time your mind works in the "yes" reaction or in the "no" reaction. "Yes" assembles; "no" dissolves.

Everything originates in mind. Begin now to school your impulses and your feelings. Your ideals are the parents of your impulses and your feelings. Whatever your ideals may have been in the past, the impulses and the feelings generated by them will be supplanted by the offspring of more sublime ideals, as these are adopted and cherished by you.

Anything now in your life can be resolved into its mental form; as a mental form it can be reduced, and finally erased. Dismissal by erasure is the one sure method of winning freedom from the undesirable. To attempt to repress is folly; the thing continues to grow, and it becomes malformed. It does not stay hidden, but comes forth, ugly and forbidding. Then you say, "I do not know why this thing came into my life. I never invited it." You consciously did not invite it, but you shaped it, and what the mind shapes will come into the manifest. Your salvation lies in erasing the causes of things unwholesome in your life. Your life is what you think:

Think straight, and life will become straight for you.

A thing that is in process of forming can be more quickly erased than a thing that has become manifest. But not always do you avail yourself of this advantage. You may be so engaged by the form-giving thought that you defer beginning the erasing process. You are fascinated by the terror of a thought-conceived calamity; you permit yourself to think that perhaps retribution will overtake someone who has displeased you. What you think concerning others takes shape in your life. Never entertain for others a thought which you would not have objectified in yourself. You are what your thoughts assemble.

You say "my mind"; another says "my mind"; every person in the world says "my mind." But there is only one mind. That mind is the Mind of God, in which individual minds have intelligence. What you call your mind is the use that you make of the Mind of God. You are intelligent to the degree in which you give the Mind of God action in you. When you receive a new idea you receive out of the Mind of God. Increase of intelligence in your mind is further disclosure of the Mind of God in you. You could not think, could not be, but for the Mind of God, as it presses upon you for manifestation.

Human intelligence has chosen a standard by which it compares individual minds. When a mind functions in accordance with that standard the mind is said to be normal. When a mind wavers from that standard it is called abnormal or subnormal. A mind that transcends that standard is super-normal.

Your mind has three fields of action. These fields are superconsciousness, consciousness, subconsciousness. To name these three fields superconscious mind, conscious mind, subconscious mind is to confuse yourself by the suggestion that you have three minds. In whatever field your mind acts, it expresses the Mind of God, interpreted by you. Superconsciousness is the Mind of God. The ideas in superconsciousness are complete, and perfect in character. You do not let their beauty appear when you modify them by your personal interpretations, dreams, and ambitions.

There is one basic fact in life which you must accept. That fact is that life in itself is perfect. There is another fact, auxiliary to the basic fact. That fact is that you can, and usually do, misunderstand and mishandle the perfectness of life. As a result, conditions do not please you. In an attempt to account for conditions you may say that life has treated you mercilessly, which is not true. You are doing the living, and your life is what you make it. You may say that God is displeased with you, which also is not true. God's relation to you is the same that it is to Jesus, but you have not profited by that relation as much as you could.

You can make your mind capable of grasping the infinite concords of life. Understanding of life begins in you when you commit yourself to the guidance of superconsciousness.

Superconsciousness is the field of inspiration. It supplies you with ideals. Its activity in the race is called progress, evolution. It contains all that has permanence. Its direct speech to you is intuition. After you have let superconsciousness speak to you until you are able to distinguish between its voice and the voice of personal desire, you need never make what even to the superficial view of life looks like a mistake.

Subconsciousness is memory, body. It is what is called race consciousness, human nature, nature. It retains the impress of all your wise and of all your unwise acts. Dispossessing the unwise things of subconsciousness by the substitution of superconscious wisdom will be the hardest work that you ever will have to do. Hardest, but unavoidable. What you do today will not have to be done tomorrow.

Consciousness plays between superconsciousness and subconsciousness. Heretofore you have been much under the dictation of subconsciousness, as it speaks in what is called natural impulse and suggestion. To control your life you must take command of consciousness, and consciously, emphatically, determine to think in accord with superconsciousness. This method, pursued without deviation, cleanses subconsciousness and prevents the accumulation of additional errors. Weakness, hurt, and what you call failure are displaced by strength, safety, and success. What you think becomes manifest.

Perception is knowledge gained through the senses. Your mind will accept the reports of the senses until you have trained it to distinguish between permanence and impermanence. Human consciousness developed the senses, and then converted them into stumblingblocks. In the work of training your mind it is imperative that you challenge every claim made by the senses, and admit only what super-consciousness approves. If you do this, the transitory will fade and the permanent will appear.

You are governed by your feeling more fully than you realize. You are swayed by likes and by dislikes. You should yield only to the truth of life that underlies all situations. When your mind veers your life veers; you become unstable, and manifestation varies. Then you say that chance or fate has overpowered you. But the statement is not true. You are being directed by your impulses; it is your life's business to direct your impulses, and so control all the issues of your life.

Will power and stubbornness are not the same. To will is to choose. Your wisest choosing will let the will of God be done in you. Never have you been able to force or to bend the divine purpose, no matter how much in human stubbornness you may have tried to defy the kingdom of heaven. That kingdom holds your good in trust; when you are willing to receive your good as good, it will be given to you. But not even you can rob you. If in the exercise of will you follow a course that contradicts the law of heaven, you later will be compelled to retrace that course, and to begin again, on the right course. You can be stubborn for a time, but eternity will find you rejoicing to do the will of Him that sent you. What you are willing to be, that you are becoming.

Power is ability to produce change. Mind is passive power; thought is active power. After you have identified yourself as the Mind of God, you begin to let God's mind manifest in you, to the exclusion of ignorance. You understand that His mind is composed of perfect, changeless ideas, and you cease to translate His ideas into imperfect, fluctuating thoughts. You know that you are what you think, and this knowledge encourages you to give way to the Mind of God.

The Mind of God pushes on your mind for expression. As you let His mind supplant what you call your mind, your thoughts change for the better. All thought is power; better thoughts than you have been using will make for you better conditions than you have been experiencing.

The changes that your mind is capable of producing range from the ultramundane to the ultraethereal. These changes may bring you from human bickerings into the communion of saints and intimacy with God. They may work wonders in your outer life, fashioning substance into myriad forms of loveliness and utility for your enjoyment. But of this one thing be assured: Intentionally or unintentionally on your part, your thoughts are changing your affairs, your body, your relationships to the world. They are changing the texture of the mental fabric which you call your mind. In this line of action your power is such that all ignorance may be banished, and your mind come to know itself.

You have as much power as anyone that ever has been on this planet or that ever will be. You are using your power, but in what way? You think, but how do you think? Perhaps you merely suppose that you think. Are you a mental parrot, imi-

tating in tone and in gesture the words, the phrases,
and the declarations of others, or are you thinking
by the power of your own mind to produce a lovelier
ideal whereby to shape a lovelier individuality? If
you never have shaped a thought, for the sake of
your own progress begin now to shape one. If need
be, take a vacation, leap your mental ruts, and blaze
your own mental trail. One thought of your own,
worked out even with labor, is better for you, more
interesting and of more value in your life than a
hundred of the most brilliant thoughts that someone
else has voiced. Be yourself; exercise your mind,
then watch yourself grow mentally. This practice
continued until it becomes a habit will make clear to
you the value of directing your thoughts, for its
effects will convince you that your mental acts are
responsible for the changes that come in your affairs.

What changes are your present thoughts destined
to bring you?

You say, "I must train my mind to think con-
structively." What do you mean by this statement?
You may take old scrap iron, old weather-beaten
boards, old broken bricks, and of them construct a
dwelling place. Your house, built from such material, will not be safe or beautiful. New, clean,
beautiful material must be used if the structure is
to be a thing of lasting beauty and usefulness. You
cannot construct a lovely and a happy life from
old, untrue, unclean thoughts. If you borrow your
thoughts you will have a life like the one whose
thoughts you use. If you let the Mind of God think
its individual thoughts in you, newness and individ-

uality will appear in you. Be sure to select the right thoughts for your building. All thoughts are constructive, in the sense that they produce their own images in the outer world.

Be sure that you want the Mind of God to think in you before saying that you let it so think. Be sure that you have placed God rather than desire in leadership over your life before you say that you are receiving the Mind of God. If you do not so prepare yourself you will make your case worse than it now is. There is no other confusion so confounding as that which comes from attributing to God the works which are the fruit of your personal, selfish thoughts.

When you become willing that your human designs may fail in order that the divine designs may prosper, you are prepared to receive from the Mind of God. Previous to that you receive from your own mind. You say, "I have been praying for approval on a course I marked out; the approval was a long time in coming, but now I know that God sanctions my plan." In an instance of this nature you perhaps receive approval from your own consciousness. It is easy to mistake desire for the will of God, and easy to misapprehend the source of approval of desire. Be watchful that you do not pray to your own consciousness and receive answers to your prayers out of your own consciousness. If ever you have felt assured of receiving what you asked and then failed to receive, the assurance of receiving came from your own consciousness, worked upon by your desire. God does not promise and then withhold. If ever you have felt assured, proceeded on your way, and then been hurt, puzzled, halted, the assurance on which you acted came from your own consciousness. God does not punish you. He does not hand you a hot poker to burn your hands by way of giving you a lesson, no matter how much you may storm and weep for the poker. When you have stormed and wept yourself into believing that after all the poker is your poker, you seize it, and at once your repentance begins. God gives you the Godly thing, which bears no fruit of hurt in your life. You give yourself the human thing. If hurts follow, you, not God, are the author of your suffering.

Until you have cleansed your mind of human desire your one prayer should be that human desire may be washed out of your soul. If human desire had made you happy and wise all these generations I would not tell you to cleanse yourself of it. But it has made you unhappy. It is the source of all that troubles you. Be sane in your prayers. Do not ask to be made able to defy life and to prosper in your defiance; ask for the wisdom that will enable you to ask wisely. The prayer will be granted; then you will have less need to "demonstrate."

Pray that you may no longer desire to desire your own will. That prayer will erase from your consciousness the wish to control yourself in your relation to God. You ask me, "Would you not control your own life?" Only to the point where I am able to surrender it to God. I know that He in me is wiser than I of myself ever can become; I know that His love will take better care of me than I can specify. So instead of wanting to control my life I want God to control it. And I know that, surrender as fully as I can, there still will be left in me enough of the personal to sustain physical identity.

In training your mind, do not ask it to contradict common sense. An intelligent orchardist does not plant a persimmon tree, then solemnly in "treatment" address it, "I affirm that you shall produce oranges." He does not plant an apple tree and then affirm, to convince himself, that the tree shall bear apples. Being intelligent, he plants an orange tree when he wishes to grow oranges; he knows that he will receive apples from an apple tree. He understands that mind has forms of expression and he knows that in all cases the form indicates the fruit to be borne. He works with the trend of mind, not against it.

If you work with the trend of mind your life will be fruitful. In you one particular form of expression is nearer to the surface than all others. That form must express first, then, after it, all others in the order of their precedence. Do not try to disarrange the order of manifestation. Do not ask your plum tree to produce peaches. To insure order, you must think coherently. To produce finished results, you must think to a conclusion.

Do not let your thoughts riot. In any chosen line of meditation or study, put all the force of order into your thinking. If your thoughts become disorderly, handle them in a manner similar to that in which a policeman lines up a crowd that seeks to crash through a doorway. Say to the thoughts that come stampeding forward, "Stand back; get into line. You may express when your time comes, but not before." This training will cause your thoughts to respond to your demand, and you will find logic becoming prominent in your thinking. You will begin to see that you are in command of your life, and that you will become what you cause your mind to do and to be.

Harness your moods. Make them work for you. They embody great power. Uncontrolled, they are undependable, weakening. Right use of moods will make you strong.

You do not have to wait on time or on inspiration, in any work. You can do as well at one time as you can at another. Time always is yours; inspiration is continuous. Work by the rule of ever-readiness, and you will become able to command ideas that remind you of your identity. You always will be in a mood to do your best. "Temperament" is mental alcoholism; it spurs and it drugs. If you would know your mental power, discard temperament. Stability and regularity will become your aim when you understand that your mental habits are also your life habits.

If you could use an instrument that would record your day's thinking and at evening repeat to you all that you had thought, you would learn why some days go amiss and why affairs sometimes are snarled. Mingled with the sweet and the true, there would be nonsensical, light, irrelevant, selfish, critical, fearful thoughts. You would behold yourself as a mental chameleon, taking on color from your environment. If you could see your thoughts materialize, as they do without your seeing the process of materialization, you would know why your affairs are unstable.

Do not habitually make excuses for your shortcomings. Face them; learn where you were remiss; then do not make those mistakes again. Do not try to stand better with people than you do with your own conscience. You may deceive your associates for a time, but you gain nothing by the deception. "You can fool some of the people all of the time, and all of the people some of the time, but you cannot fool all of the people all the time." You do not fool God any of the time, so why go to the work of framing excuses? Use your energy to correct the fault; then excuses will not be needed. Then you will have a consciousness of honesty.

If you are criticized, examine the criticism honestly, to see how much of it is justified. If you find that you are criticized for a thing which accords with your convictions, you will understand that the criticism is unavoidable. If you are unjustly criticized, accused falsely, you can afford to be lenient, not having done the thing for which you are criticized. Never let criticism induce in you a feeling of martyrdom. One who is meekly puffed up by a sense of martyrdom surely must furnish merriment for the angels.

Your mind will do for you anything that you ask of it. It will reveal to you hourly the thing that you need to know for that hour. It can be made so responsive that it will act for you at any given time, in any prescribed way. Let me tell you how I have proved this fact, many times. The relàting of one circumstance will cover all the experiences that come under the statement:

For a number of years I supplied copy for several departments in two magazines. In addition to this work I kept office hours that were long and engrossing. My writing had to be accomplished in the evenings or during week ends. Knowing that my mind would prepare the work in advance, I made a habit of setting a time in which to write a specified manuscript. I would say:

"Now, Lord, you know that we are going to need copy for such-and-such a department. We'd better do that this week end, don't You think?"

I would give the matter no further thought until the week end came. Then I would go to my desk, assemble my writing material, and begin. Not once did the theme or the development of the theme lag. Each came as easily as a conversation on a familiar subject. Many times not only the necessary manuscript would be prepared, but others, to be used later, would follow. My mind responded to my reliance on it.

Your mind responds to your reliance on it. If a matter seems difficult, brood lightly upon it; look at it; muse over it. Then put it away in the place where the Mind of God begins to become your mind. Leave it there for a season. You will find, on taking up the matter again, that it has become clear to you. This response of mind to demand was revealed to me at a time when I knew no more of metaphysics than the mere word. The experience is here related:

I was asked to prepare and read a paper before a convention. I consented, rather eagerly excited; it was my first invitation of that nature. Then arose the question, "What is your theme?" I did not know; I could think of nothing that seemed suitable. Days passed, the convention date was drawing warningly close, and still no theme came forward. A number of times I asked, "Of what shall I write?"

One day, alone in the house, I again asked the question. The theme responded instantly. Clearcut, encouraging, it announced itself by title. I said, "Right; but what shall I say on the subject?" Four subtitles, as definite and as promising as the general title, came, at once. I could not then go to my desk. In a few days I was free to write; the paper was produced at one sitting.

In training your mind, there are three facts for you to accept. These facts must be dwelt on until the one needed becomes your instant response to any unfavorable appearance for which it is the corrective. The facts are in amendment and elucidation of teachings that you may have already accepted. The facts, broadly stated:

1. You have been taught that God lives in you. The teaching is true; but it does not tell you why you live. You live because of the facts named here: God is life. Life lives; it lives itself. The life of God lives itself as you; it lives you.

2. You have been taught that the Mind of God is the only mind there is. The teaching is true, but it has not been given the expansion that would make

it comprehensible to you. The expansion that makes
the statement comprehensible is: God is mind. The
Mind of God thinks; it thinks itself. The Mind of
God thinks itself as you; it thinks you.

3. You have been taught that your thoughts
make your life. The teaching is but a partial truth,
and it does not explain the truth that it asserts. It
does not trace the unseen to the seen. The primal
facts regarding manifestation are: Thought is an
action of mind; it is the genetic entity of form. In its
beginning it is incorporeal; by continuation it becomes corporeal. It gathers substance into the shape
that is called matter. Your thought is your mind and
it is the physical entity that thinking assembles. You
are what you think.

Face life and its situations with courage. You
can unform and reform; you can bring new shapes
of good from the treasury of your mind. The world
is yours. Heaven is yours. All power is yours.

You are your own thoughts made manifest.

*I am what I think. I think life. The life of God
is released in me, and I am alive forevermore.*

*I am what I think. I think the Mind of God. The
Mind of God is released in me, and I am wise with
His wisdom.*

*I am what I think. I think power. The power of
God is released in me, and I am daily changed into
a likeness truer to Him.*

YOUR CONSCIOUSNESS
Chapter 3

Consciousness is direct knowledge or perception of an object, state, or sensation.

If you look at a tree and think of the tree while you look at it, you are conscious of the tree. In certain weather conditions, you say, "The day is blisteringly hot." You then are conscious of heat. When you enter a dark room, you are conscious of darkness; when you turn on the light, you become conscious of light.

Consciousness may be of that which the senses cannot report. You may be conscious of fear, courage, hate, and love. The sources of these feelings may be so remote from your perception that you cannot determine where the feelings have beginnings. When your consciousness is disassociated from physical sources, you are more fully identified with mind than when your consciousness is associated with an object presented by your senses. In the one instance, your mind is conscious only of a state that it has produced; in the other instance, your mind is conscious of the sense object, and it is conscious of its reactions, by which it produces a state of consciousness. Thought reactions to a given stimulus group themselves in a relationship that always is suggested by the stimulus; the group always suggests the stimulus. Sensations of pain from a burn by a live coal are repeated in your mind at the sight of a live coal. When memory vividly repeats the sensation of the burn produced by the live coal, a live coal

is suggested to your mind. The odor of roses induces
a mental picture of roses. Roses, even at a distance,
awaken memory of rose odors; while you look at
them you are conscious of their perfume, as you
are when you physically inhale their perfume.

A group of related thoughts is spoken of as a
consciousness or as a state of consciousness. The
consciousness is designated according to the character of the thought group. As, your knowledge, experience, and appreciation, having to do with art,
constitute your art consciousness. Your knowledge,
experience, and appreciation, having to do with any
one fact in life, constitute your consciousness of that
fact.

Groups of related thoughts form about every
topic that your mind considers. There are two dis-
tinctive groups with which you have to deal when
you take up the work of governing your life. One
of these groups is called the material consciousness;
the other group is called the spiritual consciousness.

The material consciousness consists of a group
of thoughts associated in a way that keeps the material aspects of life foremost in your thinking. Your
material aspect of life is your total of knowledge
concerning body, earth, human endeavor. If you rely
on this aspect of life your consciousness is material.
The spiritual consciousness is a group of thoughts
that presents the spiritual nature of life. Your spiritual aspect of life is your total of knowledge concerning God, Christ, spiritual endeavor. If you rely on
this aspect of life your consciousness is spiritual. One
of these groups may engage your attention at one

time; the other group may claim your consideration at another time. At the time in which the material group holds sway, you are in a material consciousness; when the spiritual group dominates, you are in a spiritual consciousness. If the total appeal of the material group exceeds the total appeal of the spiritual group, you have a material consciousness. If your spiritual thoughts are numerous enough, strong enough, and yoked snugly enough to outface your material thoughts, you have a spiritual consciousness.

Your consciousness is your life.

Your knowledge or perception of objects, states, or sensations is the world in which you live. You are encompassed by what you see, physically and mentally. You live in a small, mean world, if your perceptions are small, mean. You live in a large, generous world, if your perceptions are large, generous. Your mental realm is as definite as your physical realm. You live in your consciousness.

The things of which you most commonly and most ardently think become your consciousness. Because this is true, you are responsible for what you have about you. Do you know the character of your consciousness? If your group of material thoughts and your group of spiritual thoughts should instantly take on three-dimensional form and stand before you, which group would be the stronger? In which group would your thoughts of life be found? Where do you think your thoughts of finance would appear? In which association should you look, were you to search for your health thoughts? With which array

would you find your conceptions of love? Examine
your two groups; you can determine without the
aid of a seer whether your predominating consciousness is spiritual or material. Knowing which group
prevails, frequently remind yourself that your consciousness is your life. This will keep you alert to
the need of construction or reconstruction, in accordance with the chosen aim of your life.

You are either disintegrating or fortifying your
present consciousness. You are developing the consciousness which your trend of thought indicates.
You can develop any consciousness that you think
is for your greatest advantage. Mind always is the
maker.

Your mind stands between the spiritual you and
the physical you. Through your mind pours the Mind
of God, which you modify by your feeling. The
modifications that you make become parts of your
mental furnishings. They have influence with you
until their inadequacies show you that they are not
reliable sources of inspiration. Your consciousness,
even when highly spiritualized, is not to be regarded
as your leader. It is meant to sustain you, not to
prompt you. It aids and comforts you, but it never
creates. Being the product of your thinking, it never
can be the exalted source of ideas. It is your realization of the presence of God, but its voice is not the
voice of God.

If your consciousness seems to be balanced between spirituality and materiality, watch your reaction when a crisis occurs. If at the crisis your thought
leaps to God as your deliverer, you are building a

consciousness that will be so highly protective that it will disperse assault against you before assault can be organized.

While there are but two classifications of consciousness, your mind may function so almost wholly in abstractions and intellections that the product may be called a mental consciousness. This consciousness has connection with the one or with the other of the two classifications. At times it is compelled to choose its deliverer. Its choice reveals the thought group with which it is allied.

In choosing the consciousness that you mean to cultivate, ask yourself these questions: Is God or is materiality powerful? Does God or does materiality give peace? Will God or will materiality provide a field for unlimited development? Your reactions to these questions will dissipate the uncertainties that may have diverted you from a decision; they will convince you of which consciousness should claim your allegiance and your effort.

If heretofore you have drifted, your making choice of a consciousness to be attained will give a new impulse to your life. If you really are interested you will work, as you worked to secure the desirable business position that you now occupy. You will have to work to hold yourself and to strengthen yourself in your chosen consciousness, as you have to work to hold your business position and to increase your satisfactory relations therewith.

No theme yields all that it contains until it is developed in the spiritual, the mental, and the physical. God accommodates Himself to clay, and in so

doing presents to you your knottiest problems. Life,
as you now know it, reaches into the unsounded
depths of the spiritual; it explores the amazing
labyrinths of the material. Life, as you now know it,
is the starting point for your better understanding
of life.

You know that you have the power of mind to
produce any change that your consciousness demands. The power of your mind is identical with all
other forms of power. For your encouragement,
make a survey of power as you see it operating in
the world. While you are doing this, remember that
material forms of power are the outgrowth of mental
power. From the creation of the universe in stupen-
dous total to the smallest detail of the daily changes
that occur in your life, succession of events and procession of appearances revolve around the fiat,
"Let there be."

Your power is not an isolated potentiality. It is
a point of departure for universal power. It is associated with all forms of power, and in character
it is identical with the power that produces the swing
and the pull of the planets; that manifests in
weather, with its erosions that change the faces of
continents; that operates in tides that hasten or delay
traffic on the seas; that sings in waterfalls that turn
machinery; that crowds out one season by another
season, so clothing the earth in verdures or in snows;
that constructs the engines by which one hour's work
exceeds in effect the results of many men's toiling
through a day. Pursue these probings of power until
you have included yourself—the worker of magic in

a universe of magic. You, the "fearfully and wonderfully made," the marvelous mechanism of body and the omnipotent mind, have to your credit all of visible creation; have as your possibility the making of all the Edens that you shall care to inhabit.

Your mind is the recipient and the dispenser of power. It distributes the power that it receives from the Mind of God.

If you will train your thoughts by close consideration of the foregoing suggestions, you will in a measure become aware of your power. Then you will be ready scientifically to develop the consciousness that is your aim. Indifference will be supplanted by zeal; lethargy will give way to swift activity.

A specific example will serve to show how consciousness is augmented in any chosen field of knowledge. Let us trace the way by which you can develop knowledge and perception in the world of geology:

Study the works of the accredited authorities. Read slowly, that you may comprehend the ideas. Reread, ponder, digest. Be practical in your study: Compare the facts stated in your textbooks with the record of facts as you can trace them in the earth. Review the changes that occur on the surface and in the interior of the earth; meditate on the power that produces these changes. Keep in mind that the earth still is being made.

Steep your mind in your subject. You will find that ideas not presented in the text will disclose themselves to you. Give these ideas receptive attention. Newton did that in the incident of the

apple, and the world has been the wiser for the
courtesy that he showed the thought. If related subjects present themselves, make them welcome; consider them; they will explain themselves. You will
begin to feel the majesty of the universe; you will
find yourself at home in it. The mechanism of the
heavens will become intelligible to you, and you
will become familiar with wonders. All knowledge
is related, and from a fallen leaf you will become
able to read the story of space and universes.

Whatever your theme, the method by which you
arrive at understanding is the same. Study with these
two facts in mind: The textbook suggests the knowledge that at some level now lies in your mind;
study induces a flow of thought. The flow of thought
draws into your consciousness knowledge of which
you hitherto have been unconscious, and the facts
that always have existed in your mind become apparent to you.

If you wish to establish a spiritual consciousness,
you perhaps will do less perusing of books and will
give more attention to meditation. More of the spirit
of worship will characterize your application. But
you must train your thought power to act steadily,
and you must consistently adhere to your theme. Results are as sure in the one case as in the other.

Thinking clarifies ideas. Make yourself think.
You are not really thinking when you are repeating
the thoughts of others; you are parroting. To receive ideas you must keep open passage between
your mind and the Mind of God. You preserve your
mental integrity when you do not let yourself be

swayed by all that you hear or read. But mere resistance to what you hear or read does not preserve your mental integrity. Never accept a statement because an acknowledged authority has formulated it; never reject a statement because of its authorship. Compel your mind to consider, weigh; to accept or to reject. This course will produce a definite and a dependable consciousness.

To think independently of the authority that you are studying, and even in opposition to his argument, will make you mentally resourceful. In one period of my student activities I pursued the following line of action:

When the presentation of the theme supported my belief, I took the opposing side of the argument and offered all the challenges that I could produce. Then, in rebuttal of the arguments that I had made to oppose my own belief, I combined with the author's arguments all the additional points that I could muster. I did this to strengthen my ability to support my belief, in the face of any opposition that might arise.

If my belief was in opposition to the author's belief, I did all that I could to strengthen his arguments. Then I proceeded to break down the author's arguments and the arguments that I had offered in support of his. My intent in this was to fortify my mind in every way that would increase my ability to meet any argument that the question might suggest. I read for three purposes: to put an edge on my mind, to induce thought, and for the truth involved. After a few years of this practice the gaps

in a treatise loomed as obvious as an open door of a
barn, the inconsistencies as prominent as a lath-and-
plaster patch in a marble wall. I became better acquainted with my mind and I learned how to de-
clare it more concisely.

The kingdom of God is the fullness of the spiritual consciousness. The One who understood the
kingdom of God and the life of man, said that if
you seek God's kingdom and God's righteousness all
your needs will be met. You may have interpreted
that declaration in a way which leads you to con-
clude: I will seek the kingdom of God, because by
doing that I shall be benefited in material ways.
It seems to be a quick way of obtaining what I
want.

That is not what Jesus said; it is not what He
meant. If you have your mind on the material benefits that come after the kingdom has been found,
you seek the material benefits, and not the kingdom. You do not enter the kingdom. The benefits
of the kingdom do not survive removal from the
kingdom. So in seeking the kingdom merely to receive its benefits you neither enter the kingdom nor
lastingly possess its benefits.

What Jesus intended you to understand is that
as your consciousness is, so is your world. You
may respond to this teaching that you have a special, an urgent need, and that developing a new
consciousness may be slow work. You say, "I want
to be healed, now." You have a right to wholeness,
and the spiritual consciousness contains health for
you. In seeking only healing, you are not seeking

the kingdom. After you are healed you may say, "I want to be prospered." You have a right to prosperity, and the spiritual consciousness includes prosperity. After you have been prospered you may say, "I want peace." The spiritual consciousness is peace.

If you seek God in fragments you will have to return time after time, and while you are "demonstrating" your new blessing you may let the old blessing slip. All blessings are ready for you; all that God is or has is ready for you. It takes no more work to develop the spiritual consciousness in entirety than it does to "demonstrate" a single one of all the blessings that in union constitute the spiritual consciousness.

You can have the whole kingdom for the work required to gain one of its benefits. Since you can have all for the price of one, why not work for all and rejoice in all?

When you want God more than you want anything else, you will find Him. He will embolden you to press beyond the boundaries at which hitherto confidence and understanding have hesitated. The achievements of the past have no livingness for you. Let him who will, limit his soul and God. For you there is the free range of the universe; for you there is the presence of God in steady challenge to your capacity to receive. What you incorporate of God becomes your consciousness. Let God demonstrate Himself in you.

You never will establish a spiritual consciousness if you insist on separating life into parts. You cannot expect to be clear in mind concerning the

presence of God if you exclude Him through confidence in materialism. The thoughts that constitute
material consciousness ignore God. To ignore God
is not to abolish Him. No matter what barricades you
put between yourself and God, you still have God
with whom to reckon. No fact in life is rendered
null and void by your refusal to acknowledge it and
to work with it. At some point in experience you
will have to face God in a way fully as significant
as that pictured by the old theologies. Your only
defense against God is God Himself. Incorporate
God into yourself. Then you can match Him, God
to God.

The thoughts of the spiritual consciousness acknowledge God. Acknowledgment of Him brings
you assurance of His attending power and safety.
Then, when you are faced with a question that under
other circumstances would prove difficult, out of the
spiritual thought group comes to your assistance the
idea of which you have need. It says, "Here I am;
use me." In following this course no mistake occurs.

You have found the silence a means of increasing your spiritual conceptions of life. Merely keeping still is not the silence. Mere outer quietude is
not the silence. The true silence excludes materiality,
and is therefore a state of spiritual consciousness. The
true silence arrests thinking; in it you merge with
God. You do not enter the silence, for the silence
is in you. It is the center, where God is conscious of
Himself in you. Then you become conscious of the
fact that God is conscious of Himself in you. Then
comes the fusion of spiritual, mental, physical; all

manifestations are called back into the center. This is the achievement of the divine composite: "I in them, and thou in me."

You will have the right kind of confidence in yourself when you have developed a consciousness of your identity with God, His identity with you. Encompass yourself with the certainty of God and His presence, and you never will doubt your permanence and your stability as a part of the universe.

Paul expressed his assurance of God's presence in the words, "In him we live, and move, and have our being." This is a correct concept of God's encompassing presence. But it omits mention of a relation with God yet more vital. You are God-encompassed, and you are God-encompassing. To complete the unity indicated, the declaration made by Paul must be amplified in this manner: *In God you live, and move, and have your being. In you God lives, and moves, and must be given expression.* You cannot exist in God if He does not exist in you. Interdependence, reciprocity, obtain in all spheres of being. Whatever is without also is within. Unity insures this.

Efforts have been made to grade and to catalog the sins of humanity. Excessive punitive assessments for your sins have been attributed to God. You have been told that your sufferings are penalties imposed for your having broken the law. The teaching is erroneous. You are not powerful enough to break the law. You may bruise and break yourself by throwing yourself against the law, but with your mightiest efforts you cannot so much as bend the law.

You cannot, as you may say, "Set the law into action." The law always acts; nothing can halt it. The best that you can do is to give your affairs to the law; it will adjust errors.

You always act. When your act does not parallel the action of the law, you do not stop the law; you fail to avail yourself of its omnipotence. You put yourself out of unison with the celestial harmonies. Nonconformity to the law produces the wrench in consciousness that is called death. It closes your consciousness against God, who is life. Death is not the execution of God's judgment; it is the effect of God-exclusion.

Death will come to any part of your consciousness that you close against God. Belief in death closes your total consciousness against God. Fear of death is reaction to the feeling that death destroys identity. Belief in death coupled to fear of death produces irrational reactions. You say that you want to live while you live; that you will be a long time dead. Then in an effort to live while you live, you proceed to live in a way that will shorten your life. These irrational reactions do not occur after you have established your identity as an idea in the mind of God. Then you know that you live; that you are as alive as your consciousness; that to expand consciousness is to expand life.

Your reaction to the thought of death may spur you to a course of living which you believe will, as it is expressed, enable you to attain eternal life. Work to attain eternal life is superfluous. Life is eternal. The eternal life of God is all the life there is. Your work is to attain an eternal consciousness of life.

The fierce demand of your heart to know life, the insistent appeal of your soul for assurance of conscious survival in all experiences, are prophecy of a knowledge to come. Some day you will know your immortality. Knowledge of immortality is contained in spiritual consciousness. The Mind of God yields what you seek in it. Environ yourself with spiritual ideas and thoughts: live in God; so merge yourself with Him that you feel Him living what you have been calling your life. You will feel your consciousness becoming God's consciousness, and the certainty of endless survival with Him will give you abiding peace.

Do you sometimes pray, "O God, pour out Yourself upon me"? If you do, your picturization of the experience must be that of God immediately above you, pouring down His essence on you. Such an experience as that never has occurred in the life of anyone. It will not occur for you. The positions are wrong. It is true that God is above you; He also is beneath you and around you. But from none of these points does He pour out Himself for you. Whatever of Himself God pours for you is poured out in you and through you, outward. Your vital contact with Him comes from your touching His inner presence. Within, He pours out Himself as you, spiritually; through you, mentally; sustaining you, physically. Not the life in the orchard but the life in the individual tree produces the fruit of the tree. When you know where you contact God you are in the relation to Him that enables you to receive His outpouring

of Himself. Then He releases Himself in you, and
you are blessed in every way.

A landowner in a desert finds a spring issuing
from a hill. He cuts a larger opening for the pent
waters that have been trickling forth. A little strip
of desert becomes verdured; the landholder again increases the size of the aperture through which the
water flows; he digs lateral trenches and conducts
the water to various areas. He now has a green farm
in the midst of the desert grayness. He continues to
enlarge the opening of the spring, and increasing
acreage of productive farm land is the result.

The spring is the junction of your mind with
the Mind of God. The desert is your consciousness
before you knew how to redeem it. Let God flow
out. Life in you will become alive, beautiful, productive.

Do not let yourself be abashed by the statement
that you can become conscious of God in you, doing
His perfect work. Do not become over-emboldened
by it. Be sensible, confident, modest. The spring
flows increasingly for you when you enlarge the
outlet. Make no comparisons between your life and
the lives of others. Let God's mind think you. Let
God's life live you. When your thought dwells on
the mighty works of those who have known how to
let God express, say, "Since God has done this thing
in another, He will do it in me when my receptiveness to Him matches the receptiveness of the one in
whom He has already done this work." Do not measure your life by the life of another; steady your
thoughts in the consciousness that all that God re-

quires of you is to be passive to Him. Think not of the agency, but of the crowning manifestation of God, wherever and whenever it occurred; say, "Since God has done this work in one He will do greater works in me when my receptiveness to Him surpasses the receptiveness of the one in whom He has done this work."

You are the creator of your own consciousness.

My consciousness is my life.

In God I live, move, and have my being.

In me God lives, moves, and has expression.

THE REAL AND THE FICTITIOUS
Chapter 4

The *real* is that which has "actual existence"; it is "not theoretical or imaginary." The *fictitious* is that which is "imaginary, hypothetical, or false."

The real is the permanent. It continues "in the same state or without essential change." The fictitious is the impermanent; it does not continue "in the same state or without essential change."

Life is permanent; it does not change. Manifestations of life are impermanent; they change. Life is real. Manifestations of life are fictitious in the appeal that they make to you before you have learned to distinguish between cause and effect. They do not support your expectations of them; they seem to promise much, but if you rely on them, they fail you. Nevertheless, during the term of their continuation, they are actual and accurate representatives of their origins. Their inconsistencies are not in themselves but in you, who expect permanence of impermanence.

If you spiritually are in a state of amnesia, the fictitious will first claim your attention. You will see manifestation unassociated with its origin, and you will be puzzled in your efforts to account for it. If manifestation is pleasing, you will be content. If manifestation is unpleasing, you will be dissatisfied. Conscious only of manifestation is Adam of the Scriptures—glad for the apple, gloomy when caught. If you accuse outside parties of responsibility for your predicament, you continue in the

Adam line of action. You make your helpmeet a
hindrance. Manifestation is a warning or it is an
encouragement; it never should be regarded as an
advisor or as an end to be sought.

"In Adam all die." All that is in the fictitious,
all that is imaginary, all that is counterfeit, all that
is false, will disintegrate. All that is impermanent
will permanently vanish. All reliance on manifestation will cease.

If you have regained consciousness of your spiritual identity you will know that manifestation
changes with the changes that take place in your
mind. You will know how to ally yourself with
realities, never again to be misled by fictions.

"In Christ shall all be made alive." The senses
are accurate within their own ranges, but their ranges
are so circumscribed that you cannot from the senses
alone gain any appreciable knowledge of reality.
There are vast universes of being that the senses
do not touch, and in order not to be deceived you
must have a more capable guide, a more compre-
hensive reporter of events than the senses ever can
be. The fictions that perplex you are the discrepancies
between the reports of the senses and the facts of
life that exist beyond the reach of the senses. You
have innate knowledge of all the facts of being.
But when contradictions arise between innate knowledge and the senses, you say that you cannot believe
what you see. You can believe what you see, but
you may make the mistake of trying to stretch sight
into realms that the eyes cannot penetrate.

Christ, as exemplified in Jesus of Nazareth, is

the redemptive power of your mind; the real; the
permanent. Christ awakens all the realities; reveals
the permanent. All your innate beauty, all your holy
aspirations, all your eternal relationships with life
and love and good, are made alive. Dormant power
is aroused. Truth, buried beneath fiction, is resur-
rected. In Christ, the life of God manifesting, you
are made alive consciously, to live forevermore.

The real and the fictitious blend in ways that
may make them look indistinguishable to you. The
ground under your feet is real in that it is not merely
a concept or a conjecture. It is fictitious in that it is
an imitation of what the personal mind believes to
be a support and a field of activity for all of life.
It is permanent in the sense that it does not fail you
in the uses for which it was constructed. It is impermanent in the sense that in it change is constant.
The horizon is real because it is not theoretical; it is
fictitious because it is but an apparent meeting of
earth or sea and sky. It is permanent because it will
endure as long as the world endures; it is impermanent because it changes with the changing position of the observer.

The real and the fictitious join where primary
cause transmutes into effect. Primary cause is mind;
effect is the form created by your personal use of
mind. Primary cause is eternal reality. Effect is eternally fictitious: the swaying shadow of the wind-
moved tree; the mask at the ball; the image in the
pool.

Knowledge of what you are includes knowledge
of the real and of the fictitious. When you see a

shadow you know that it does not exist of itself; you know that it is cast by a body, familiar or unfamiliar to you. The relation between body and shadow, in the less obvious aspects of life, becomes clear to you, and you perceive that you have consciousness of two worlds. One world is real. One world is fictitious.

The real world is the world in which God is recognized. The fictitious world is the world in which God is not recognized.

You are native to the real world; in it you have union with God; in it you have sustenance and eternal being. But you do not consciously live in the real world all of the time. You adventure into the fictitious. You wrestle with its shadows; you plead with its irrationalities; you clasp its phantom forms to your bosom, to extract rest from their restlessness. You deceive yourself so thoroughly that you finally cease to remember what you are; you become a victim of spiritual amnesia.

Having recovered consciousness of your identity, you return to your home, the real world. In the real world you recognize God as He is, and not as you thought Him to be while you were lost in the fictitious world.

You do not recognize God when to Him you attribute motives and acts contrary to His nature. If you say, "God has afflicted me," you do not recognize Him. Affliction is the shadow of a foolish gesture; it does not come from God. If you say that God's plan for you includes hardships of any sort, you do not recognize Him. God is the blessed and the good; you live in Him. God is the beautiful and the joyous; He lives in you. The imperfect thing is an ugly mask; changes are the images of objects that pass above the pool. In the fictitious world you use God. In the real world God uses you. When you use God manifestation fails you, mocks you, hurts you. When God uses you manifestation sustains you, encourages you, soothes you.

In the fictitious world you experience death, sickness, poverty, sorrow. In the real world you possess, know, and rejoice in life, health, opulence, happiness. The fictitious world offers you its all, but its all cannot enrich you. Its promises are as the promises of the mirage lake that lies alluringly ahead, but the eager traveler never tastes the refreshing coolness of its tantalizing waves.

How can you judge between the real and the fictitious? The Mind of God in you knows. Let it choose.

A story in the Talmud relates that the Queen of Sheba, to test the wisdom of Solomon, came into the monarch's presence, carrying a bouquet in each hand. One bouquet was of real flowers, the other was the finest product of the imitator's art. So true to each other in appearance were the two bouquets that great Solomon could not decide the question propounded by the queen. As he pondered he noticed bees outside the casement; he ordered the windows to be opened; the bees entered and flew to the flowers held by the queen's right hand. Then those present knew, as fully as wise Solomon knew, which flowers were real, which were imitation.

Your innate intelligence will find the real for you. It will testify of things eternal. Open your consciousness to it. Let it judge. Trust it.

The real is substance; the fictitious is shadow. What the real possesses the fictitious claims; what the real is the fictitious assumes to be.

Manifestation is not evil; it is not error. It is the consistent outpicturing of the inconsistent human consciousness. On its apparent inconsistencies have been based all judgments against it. In any form it is not real in the sense that it exists of itself. In any form it ceases when the sustaining force of consciousness is withdrawn, and it appears as the new form that the changed consciousness assembles and maintains.

The element of duration is found in the fictitious world and in the real world. In the fictitious world duration is time; in the real world duration is eternity.

If you have not recovered consciousness of your spiritual identity you are more aware of time than of eternity.

Time is the thread of experience on which you string the beads of events. Time is a Janus, one face looking forward, one face looking backward. The forward look is future time; the backward look is past time. Present time, or now, is minimized in the fictitious world.

The future shelters apprehension: Crops may fail; you may lose your position; old age is coming. Fear of these things paralyzes you. Like a charmed bird you flutter and protest before the devouring snake of time. You think no deliverance possible. You vision evil, you expect grief. And events, the progeny of your mind, are delivered of your mind into the outer world. A mother whose three sons were in penal institutions told me that while her children were yet but babes she saw them committing the crimes for which as men they were incarcerated in prisons. That mother worked in the fictitious world; she accepted results before they appeared; she did not know how to rear her sons in the righteousness and the safety of the real world. Had she known that the real world can be made to blot out the figures of the fictitious world, she could have dissolved the mental nebula in her children that later emerged as act in the area of manifestation.

The future lures you with anticipations. But its promises are handcuffed to postponement. You think, "I will be great tomorrow." You cannot be great tomorrow if you do not begin to be great today. You do not have to wait until tomorrow for the things that would be lovely for you today. What is not now ready for you never will be ready for you. Nevertheless, all that you can think is now ready for you. Beyond what you can think or feel or dream, the scope of God expands with enrichment for you. Why wait?

Your past is your array of regrets, sorrows, indorsements, compliments. Memories of regrets and sorrows often are less inhibitive of growth than are memories of indorsements and compliments. If you give attention to past triumphs, you neglect your present opportunity for better triumphs. You should be wiser, stronger, more splendid now than you ever were in the past. Burn the old laurels and earn new ones. Make this day your supreme day. By so doing you will transcend the inhibitions that memories of personal events entail.

Cease to be proud of former weaknesses, or you will become more weak. Cease to be proud of ancestors, and achieve honor for yourself. An honorable line of ancestry attests high-minded companionship, but the line will deteriorate if you do not keep your life honorable. You can, but you may not, secure the past by the present. Evolution halts or hastens in you. Ancestry is neither a liability nor an asset. Your life is an individual responsibility, an individual opportunity.

Be little concerned with your grandfather's behavior; be greatly concerned with the behavior of his grandson. Physical ancestry is a convenience. Mental ancestry is a necessity. In all vital ways you are your own ancestor. What you were in former times has produced the you of today. The you of today begets the you of tomorrow. To improve the product, the you of today must transcend the you of yesterday.

Time is unknown in the real world. If you try to speak of that world in terms of time, you must say that it was, that it is, that it will be, changelessly itself. Your correct thought is expressed in the world *now.*

The *now* of continuous consciousness is the eternity of the real world. Observe: I find you holding a book. I ask, "Why not read?" You answer, "I have been reading, but now I am thinking over a statement I found in the book." If yesterday I had met you on the street and asked you where you were going, you might have said, "I am going to the post office, now." Tomorrow I may ask you what you are doing, and you may answer, "I now am packing to go out of town."

You draw on your memory, and say, "I now remember." You anticipate, and say, "Now I wonder if my effort will be as successful as I hope." In the past moment you said "now"; in the present moment you say "now"; in the moment to come you will say "now." In so speaking you accord with the real world. Eternal consciousness of life operates in *now*. The tick of eternity's clock says, *"Now, now; now, now."*

Time inhibits. You look back at an event and you say, "That was a long time ago." Then you begin to feel old. A feeling of old age includes a feeling of inability. You look forward, in computation of your remaining time in the fictitious world, and you say, "My grandfather lived to be eighty; my mother made the transition at seventy; I still have perhaps thirty, perhaps twenty years." Then your thoughts begin to shrivel; your body takes up the mental cue and acts upon it. You feel that life has to do with time. But you are wrong. Experience has to do with time. Life has to do with eternity.

Years do not make you old. Years are your accumulation of experiences. You are the identity that you were before birth. That identity never is taken from you. The man of eighty years experience is the same man that he was at the experience of sixty, forty, twenty years. Methuselah died the same identity that he was born. There is no oldest man, no old man. You do not grow old because the earth swings around the sun. What you do with the life stuff marks your body, but you are beyond the reach of age.

Life is real; age is fictitious. Get that distinction, and you will understand that age is a habit—a habit to be avoided. You will understand that years, alone, do not lessen your ability. You will understand that your regard for years is the cause of decline in your confidence toward life, and that decline of confidence marks your body with what you call age. You now should be a more capable man, a more capable woman, than you were twenty years ago.

If you say that because of years you cannot do the work that you once did, I will answer your charge against yourself by saying that life does not expect you to do the work that you once did. There is a better work for you. The only person who continues to do the work that he once did is the imbecile, who makes no progress in mind and body. Life demands growth, change, progress, of you.

If you still wish to doze in the somnolent blankets of age, you perhaps will say to me, "But you can't teach an old dog new tricks." Then I will say to you, "If the dog won't learn new tricks, he *is* an old dog, or in a way soon to become an old dog." Interest in new things is the most splendid characteristic of youth. Refusal to learn, refusal to try, produces the fossilization which, only, can be called old age.

Blessed be change. It is the flow of the living water from the living fountain of life. Blessed be the struggle to grow. It is the witness of an ever-increasing zest and capability.

Eternity releases. What time binds, eternity sets free. Your faculties expand, your soul rejoices, and your body thrills to the realization that there can be no defeat, no end; that progress is as eternal as being; that life and development are one.

Engage your thoughts in the realm of the real. Improve your mind; eternity lies before you. Lift your eyes to the golden heights of vast achievements; you live now, and you will continue to live, always. The improvements that you make in your mind fit you to meet the expanding opportunities of unrolling eternities. The victories that you gain in yourself bring you into broader concepts and give you fairer perspective of your possibilities. Now is the point of beginning the works that you have deferred because time seemed too full for all that you would do. Working with time, you never will finish what lies before you. God gives you eternity in which to perfect the perfect thing that you would do.

All that hurts you and all that annoys you are fictitious; they pass; you and your eternal opportunity remain. Poverty, sickness, death, transpire in the fictitious world; you, the *what,* go through them unscathed. Only the *who* suffers. You, the *what,* emerge, opulent, whole, alive, as you were before you entered the ordeal. You profit by the ordeal if

through all its circumstances you hold a firm consciousness of *what,* and let considerations of *who*
drop to the level of the negligible.

Take your mind off the past; let it go; it cannot
help, and it is quite sure to hinder you. If you were
lovely, popular, thirty years ago, and are not lovely,
popular, today, you have severed your connection
with the traits that made you sought for in former
years. Reconnect with those traits, and you will be
sought for today. If you treasure mementos, reread
the letters that commended you for the deeds and
graces of five years ago, you perhaps are doing so
to the neglect of those acts and ways that would
win you commendation now.

If you treasure your joys you will find it easy to
treasure your sorrows. A review of former joys is a
mode of vanity. A review of sorrows is the weak-
ling's plea for a sympathy that will further weaken
him. You say, "I have been through so much." You
are not through your sorrows if you relive them, talk
them, insist on giving them a page in your life book.
While you recount and revisualize them they are as
potent with you as they were when they occurred.
Your emphasis of them in memory may make them
more potent, for most sorrows, like most adven-
tures, grow with each review of them. Nothing that
you drag into the present is wholly in the past. If you
tie yourself to memories of events in the fictitious
world, you become as one stumblingly walking backward up the slope of endeavor, tugging at a chain
gang of ghosts. Dead things do not move of themselves. Your progress is slow while you strain to

keep your retinue in hand. The fictitious forms that people the dead years are not the marching comrades of the forward-moving mind.

Each world has its inhabitants. In the real world there are God and His idea—you. There are living potentialities, vibrant, eager. There are the hosts of good, the as yet unrevealed splendors, the vision of which Paul found not lawful to be uttered. There is work, the accomplishment of perfections of which you now have not so much as a hint. There is endless progress, on and on toward the heart of God; on, until you awake with beholding His likeness.

The fictitious world is inhabited by ghosts. Idle dreams drift through the areas of consciousness. Imaginations founded on ignorance walk with you. In that world you construct dragons, and then cower before them. Of the formless you assemble forms of terror which you permit to paralyze your mind.

I became aware of the hypnotic influence of the fictitious world in an experience which I here relate for the purpose of showing you how you may be yielding to your own imaginations:

We were three girls, in midteens. My companions asked me to tell them a ghost story. I had told them ghost stories on other occasions, but never before amid such favorable surroundings.

We were in a lamp-lit room of a small, isolated house. The night was dark, windy. Tree boughs moaned, doors shook; at intervals the air sighed eerily about the house.

With secret zest I acquiesced in their demand. I gave my imagination rein and spur. My companions began to respond; they shuddered, but still smiled. I saw that to give them the stimulation that they were expecting I should have to do better than I was doing. I did better. I heaped horror on horror. My companions ceased to smile; they cast fearful glances at open doorways to dark rooms; they clutched at each other, but eyed me expectantly.

I was much encouraged by their appreciation. I broke all bounds; possibilities were spurned and impossibilities were transcended. Gruesome situations, gruesome objects, were depicted with mounting fervor. My audience was responding most satisfactorily.

Then, all at once, without the slightest warning of the land of terrors into which my own fabrications had taken me, *I believed that story, myself.* I sat rigid, frozen by the creations of my own fantastically misdirected imagination. My companions shouted with laughter; they took hold of me and shook me to break the hideous nightmare that I had created for myself. I was dazed with relief when I realized my commonplace surroundings.

After that most successful recital I never told those girls, or anyone else, a ghost story. I had lost my taste for being entertaining in that way.

Later, I became aware that I was telling myself ghost stories of another sort. I saw that these ghost stories had an effect similar to, but not so swiftly apparent as, the effect of the story that I had concocted that dark and windy night. I closely watched results, and I found that when I told myself that I was sick, the sense of sickness increased. I found that when I told myself that I was poor, my money did not go so far, and debts appeared. I found that whenever I chose my companions from the inhabitants of the fictitious world, my energies lagged to the time of their movements, and that a state of torpor ensued. Observing these things, I resolved to tell myself no ghost stories of any sort. In addition I resolved to tell myself the truth on all occasions.

Truth is the character of things and of events that occur in the real world. Cleave to truth, though all evidence seems to support fiction. If you tell yourself the ghost story that represents yourself as incapable, you will find your mind congealing with the fear that you cannot do the thing that is for your good and for the good of others. You will have to be brought back to reality, even if your restoration must be accomplished by ridicule and figurative shakings. If you tell yourself that God's capability is your capability at all times, you will feel the warm currents of returning confidence flowing through your being. Then you will accomplish what you should.

If you tell yourself the Adam-old ghost story that you fail because of another, you will paralyze your powers of initiative, and will become an addict of the alibi. If you are large enough to acknowledge your mistake, accept the results, and then set about reforming conditions by conforming with the laws of the real world, you ultimately will find yourself a free man.

Every negative mental picture is a ghost story. Every recital of wrongs is a ghost story. Delineations of symptoms of illness are ghost stories. To relate a hard luck story is to relate another ghost story.

When you say of anything that it is too good to be true, you tell yourself a ghost story. Everything that speaks of good is true—an incident of your life in the real world. All things begin in the mind. To claim the good of which you are able to think is but simplest honesty. The act of claiming gives the thing an impulse that starts it toward you. Make your claim on the grounds of your natal rights. You are a citizen of the real world, wherein exists for you all that you can claim of the enduring, and wherein there is infinitely more than you have thought of claiming. When you have so fully identified yourself with the real that you cannot be shaken or rendered doubtful by the pretenses of the fictitious, you never will say of anything that it is too good to be true. Of the best that you can hear, of the best that is hoped, of the best that is prophesied, of the best that is revealed, and of the best that stands beyond the pale of present revelation, you will say, "It is good enough to be true."

Identify yourself with the real; the fictitious will loose its hold on you. "I will arise, and go to my Father."

You are an alien in the world of the fictitious. You are heir apparent to the splendors of the real world.

God's world is the real world.
In God's world life is eternal.
In God's world good is unending.
I live in God's world of eternal life and endless good.

LIFE PAYS
Chapter 5

D o you, in querulous mood, ask yourself
"Does life pay?"
If you do, make this candid answer every
time that the question comes into your mind: "Yes,
life pays. It pays me all that I am worth."

The question will not present itself after you
have regained consciousness of your spiritual identity. But until you have learned what you are, it frequently may arise. A rigid application of the honest
answer to the question will do you a number of
favors: It will explain itself in ways that will convince you that life plays fair. It will reveal why your
efforts do not always produce expected results. It
will make plain the challenging fact that God's wage
scale is exact, that on God's payroll, no favorites are
listed. It will show you that you cannot be paid for
your earning capacity only. It will teach you the
most important fact in the economics of the universe: life pays an accurate wage. It pays you for
what you do. More vitally than that, it pays you in
what you do.

You find about you the products of your labor.
Nothing is given to you—you get what you earn,
you earn what you get. Circumstances are not acci-
dents. Friendships are not chance-wrought. The
two and two of your endeavors equal the four of
your results. You are cause and your circumstances
are effect.

To forestall disappointments, you must be intensely honest with yourself. Do not expect more and better than you have earned; do not expect less and poorer than you have earned. Self-conceit and self-abasement are equally unfair, equally misleading. You may be advised that in order to be heard you must blow your own horn. Before acting on that advice, consider what kind of music you will produce. Persons who blow their own horns usually are poor musicians. They run a monotone on the third note of the scale—*mi, mi, mi.* This is music only to the ears of the hornblowers. Do not expect the wage of applause for such a performance.

Poise toward life is compounded of confidence and modesty. Be confident when you remember what you are. Be modest when you remember who you are. You know that you have power; you know that acting of yourself you may misuse your power. The mind that is full of its own conceits cannot find room for the activity of divine ideas. Jesus was supreme in the poise of blended confidence and modesty. When He gave His final instructions to His disciples, He confidently said, "All authority hath been given unto me in heaven and on earth." On an occasion when He was addressed as "good Master," He modestly said, "Why callest thou me good? none is good save one, *even* God."

The rule is: Let your living, not your tongue, recommend you. Self-deceptions and pretenses do not long avail. They never are wholly successful, for there is no reality in them. A presence as of insincerity accompanies one who tries to appear what he is not, but sincerity clothes the honest one as with a

holy vestment. Your living justifies a high claim or
makes a high claim ridiculous. What your living
justifies you do not have to demand. You possess by
virtue of having accomplished. The otherwise great
man is small when he boasts of his own achievements. Results announce themselves. A survey of life
will show you that all the meanness is yours, that all
the goodness is God's.

Your consciousness pervades your work, and
gives it character—your character. You are recognized as clearly by your work as you are by your
walk, your speech, your manners, your face. You
are more broadly known by your work than by your
personality; your personality is restricted, but your
work is imprinted on the substance of the universe
and recorded by the minds of men.

Respect your work; it is the expression of your
soul. It presents you to the world. It is a form of
you.

The heroes and the world characters of former
times live today in what they accomplished. Years
do not diminish but rather increase the wage of
love and gratitude bestowed upon those who work
beneficently. Time does not apologize for those who
work for the hurt of others, nor does it minimize
the nature of their deeds. It identifies the worker
with his work, and names effect for the cause of
effect. So the name Christian is properly given to
whatever is clean with the cleanness of the Christ,
and Mephistophelean is used to denote cunning devoted to debauchery.

Your work will live if it has life in it. If it has

not life in it, your work never has lived, it never can be made to live. Real work, living work, is of the real world, the world wherein God is recognized. Real work discloses yourself to yourself; it enlarges your awareness of power; it expands your mind to receive more of God. It makes you aware of the partnership that always has existed between you and God. "My Father worketh even until now, and I work," said Jesus, in declaring that the soul is to make manifest the things of God.

Your real work is the building of yourself. All effort not directed that way is auxiliary to the main endeavor. Accumulated objects of monetary value are not a gauge of your rewards in the real world. Monetary values may be as distinct from real wealth as physical strength may be distinct from moral strength. Monetary values become wholly fictitious when they are substituted for the wealth of the real world. Money or its equivalent is lawful, necessary, sure, when you rightly relate yourself to life. But to believe and to practice the belief that the success of your living is to be computed by your financial resources is to confuse values and to misdirect your efforts.

It is said that when Queen Elizabeth I was told that her time life had reached the measure of but a few hours, she cried, "Millions of gold for minutes of time!" The vain and self-willed queen had accumulated much fictitious wealth. Fortitude, courage, faith, the wages of the unselfish worker, had not been her award. Life paid her, but at the balancing of the books her assets did not sustain her or give her courage to face the possible demands of the unknown.

Monetary values are not the wages of life. They belong in another category. They relate to the fictitious. If you spend your life merely in making a living you finally must acknowledge yourself bankrupt in essential wealth. A broader, richer mind, a far-visioning and buoyant soul, a sure, a reassuring contact with the realities, are the values gained from life when you live for life and not for manifestation. Life pays. You name your recompense by what you do, by what you are.

You have much to learn. One elementary lesson is that a surface defeat may contain the germ of a transcendent success. Tests are the whetstones on which you are to sharpen the metal of your ability. I have seen this proved many times, but never more convincingly than in the case of a boy who had rounded eight years of experience when he made the discovery that a temporary check holds potential gain. The case of the boy:

John was tough-muscled, courageous, a valiant devotee of the manly art of self-defense. Sometimes he carried the manly art out of its self-defensive area into the area of offensive overtures. He was champion in his neighborhood.

One day he came home showing signs of battle, and rather the worse for the encounter. One eye was blacker than nature had made it; one cheek was redder than its usual hue; his nose presented larger proportions than the family remembered. His father said:

"You've been fighting again."

"Yes," said John. "I've been fighting."

"You mixed with the new boy in the next block."

"Yes."

"And he trimmed you," grinned the father.

"Yes, he trimmed me," admitted John, "but I got practice out of it."

If you find yourself "trimmed" by any enterprise you have undertaken, be like John, a philosopher. Get practice out of it. Your "trimmings" are not ordained for the purpose of giving you practice. You receive them because you are not yet fit to cope with the situations that you challenge. If you get practice out of them you will find yourself fit for greater matters. Practice induces growth. If you treat experiences as punishment you acknowledge outlawry in yourself. If you treat experience as practice you acknowledge yourself an apprentice training for mastership. The lad John of the story is now a man, devoting his strength and his fearlessness to bringing nature under the dominion of man, for the benefit of man.

Be the model that you think others should be. Then you always will have a standard of endeavor and attainment. The excellence that you demand should be demanded of yourself, since you have conceived that idea of excellence. Be wiser, live better, attain to sublimer heights than you expect of your teachers. Unless the pupil surpass the teacher progress will cease. Devote to better living the energy that you could spend in criticism; then your vision will become so clear that you will find nothing to criticize anywhere; your demand on yourself will be so inclusive that there will be left no space in which to harp at others.

If you live right your ability steadily will increase. Solar systems may slow down and cease. Mind never can do either. While you let the mind of God think itself in you, increase of intelligence and ability distinguishes your life.

Today in time is the fruit of your yesterdays. Tomorrow is the bud on the stalk of today. If you count progress by time, in order to be consistent you must expect the life wage to increase with the passing of years. As your business thrives and as your finances accumulate you must see to it that your mental and your moral assets also increase. Otherwise you will become a moneyed mendicant. If you count progress by improvement of consciousness, you will know how to make life richer and you will notice that your efforts exactly tally with your rewards. Then you will not bewail the passing of the years. Time and eternity, the procession of events, will not distract your attention from life. And life will reward you for your fidelity by uncovering more of itself in you.

Do not hope to trade your years for pleasures. That portion of eternity which you call time cannot be exchanged for baubles; time is your present concept of everlastingness, and your use of it is noted on your wage account. But this does not mean that life is merciless. It means that life cannot be mocked; it means that the only crop that you can reap is the crop that you sow in your consciousness.

You cannot have a spiritualized, redeemed body, without first spiritualizing, redeeming your consciousness. The incorruptible, living body of God is the essential body, from which your physical body emerges. Your essential body occupies your physical body, and your physical body will be converted into the substance of God's body as you let the body of God diffuse itself through your flesh, cleansing the atomic entities and awakening them in the resurrection of immortality.

Your essential body is the reality of which your flesh body is the three-dimensional representative. Your essential body possesses and exercises faculties that your mind has translated as organs of your physical body. The use that you give an organ may misrepresent the faculty on which the organ is based. Misuse blunts, perverts, and finally destroys the sensibility of the organ misused. Physical death follows continued or extreme misuse of any part of the physical body. But in any change that comes to your physical body your essential body is not destroyed, not even impaired.

When revealed or partially revealed, the essential body appears to the beholder as an angel or as a glorified soul. On the mount of Transfiguration, Peter, James, and John saw the essential body of Jesus. The body that was there revealed was the body which absorbed His body of the resurrection; the body so beautiful that His disciples did not recognize it; the body to which walls and barred doors were not barriers. The radiance and the amazing beauty of your essential body could persuade one

looking upon it that you might be Moses or Elijah,
an angel or an archangel. The body and the mind
of God are in you what they are in those who are
highest in the courts of heaven; they adapt themselves to your use in any realm of life.

In four instances I have witnessed transfigura-
tions, two of which occurred in one person. The
circumstances which attended these occurrences were
as described here:

I was conversing with a woman of much spiritual consecration. One who measures life by time
would not call her a young woman.

As we talked a change appeared in her countenance. There was a suffusing of lines, a forming
of a new contour. Color and expression of inde-
scribable loveliness followed. The alterations absorbed the countenance that I had known, and I
stood face to face with a glorious being. I was not
dreaming; my senses were alert; I kept my consciousness of place and circumstance; I remembered that
this splendid one was also a woman of my acquaint-
anceship. I steadily observed the apocalypse; it was
not fleeting. A number of minutes must have passed
before my attention was demanded by another.
When I again had opportunity to look at the one in
whom I had seen the transfiguration, the mask had
been drawn over the essential body and the physical
again stood forth.

A few days later, I, with two other women, called
on this woman. She had sustained a bereavement of
one extremely dear. I spoke but little, listening to
the brave words of the sorrowing one, and to the

sweet, wise words of the others. Again transfiguration began, working in the three. The change was complete in each; radiant was each with the life supernal, more than young was each in the agelessness of eternal being. From what was there opened to my vision I learned John's meaning in the statement, "And the Word became flesh, and dwelt among us (and we beheld his glory, glory as of the only begotten from the Father), full of grace and truth."

I know a woman who has been semi-invalid for years. The physical is pallid, bent, and deeply carved by sufferings, yet to me this woman always within carries the glow, the vigor, the rounded proportions, and the free, upright grace of her early womanhood.

Not one of these experiences has come as a result of my trying to bring it about. I never seek a particular experience, never visualize it, never image it.

The integrity of your effort counts. Your words, your claims, your intentions speed forward to manifestation when they are vitalized by an intense sincerity. You cannot afford to cheat yourself by assuming that you have done the work that yet remains to be done. The enterprise of righteous living demands your all. Evolution is the man's return to God. Your return is swift or slow, governed by your industry. Mind leads; the body follows the mind. By this order of procedure comes the redemption of your mind and your body. Your better understanding of life is the reward that gives you greatest happiness. Life pays; it pays by giving itself.

Life pays you in the currency of the realm wherein you operate.

If you serve in the realm of the fictitious your wage will be paid you in the spurious currency of that realm. There, where there is no livingness, you frantically struggle to accumulate the form of supply that will support you after you have let your faith in years deplete your ability. Having received your wage, you find that it does not meet your entire need. You feel that some better part is lacking; that, despite your labors and your accumulations, there is something yet to be acquired. You begin to appreciate the truth in the words, "Man shall not live by bread alone."

If you serve in the realm of the real your wage is paid you in the living currency of that realm. There, where life has everlasting dominion, you work with God in an increasing power, to produce enduring results. You amalgamate with all good; you arrive at peace. You prove the truth in the words, "Man shall . . . live . . . by every word that proceedeth out of the mouth of God."

In the realm of the fictitious you hate, and your hate brings you hate; your suspicions are returned with suspicion; your feeling of insecurity rewards you with insecurity.

In the realm of the real you love, and your love pays you with love; your trust reaps you a hundredfold increase of trust; your feeling of security becomes the fact of security.

The surest thing in life is that life pays.

When you think in accord with the real, you

automatically shut out of your consciousness all matters that pertain to the fictitious; you find that God is your companion, and that His kingdom is your home. The work of compelling your mind to think in accord with reality pays a royal wage: It causes your involuntary thinking to adjust itself to the heavenly conditions of the real world.

You do not have to receive out of the fictitious. You choose; your choice is your compensation. If someone should try to give you an infuriated rattlesnake you would not put out your hand to take the serpent. Yet you feel that you must receive and even cherish the poisonous serpents tendered you by the fictitious world. You say that pain, poverty, disappointment, and grief are mighty realistic while they last, admitting that they are not real in the sense of inherency. Well, if you grasp the serpent, there is an antidote for its bite. The antidote is the reality that you spurned for the fiction. You do not have to receive an emissary from the fictitious; you do not have to accept an offering from the fictitious. It always takes two to make a bargain. What you admit into your life from either the fictitious or the real is your pay for opening the door between you and the realm from which you receive.

"He that loseth his life for my sake shall find it," said Jesus, in speaking of the one who forsakes unreality for reality. The exchange here indicated does not involve rewards. Your act produces. Christ is the essence. Christ also is the intelligence that, acting on essence, brings together you and the kingdom of heaven. Do not work for rewards; work

to find God. Your wage will be the discovery of
God within your individuality.

The Mind of God informs you that when you
speak and act in appeal to the outer, the outer is all
that can recompense you. The recompense made by
the outer is inconstant, ephemeral. The popular idol
must cease to be himself; he must become the constant spectacular appeal that his public demands of
him. If he does not do this he is cast from his
pedestal, upon which is placed the one who more
completely forsakes himself. It cannot be otherwise.
The fictitious must maintain its fictions, and he who
does not measure to the specifications suffers eclipse.
"Had I but served my God with half the zeal I served
my king, he would not in mine age have left me
naked to mine enemies," said Wolsey in his ex-
tremity. The king to whose personal vanities and
vices the cardinal had ministered, disdained him, excluded him from royal favor, when the old church-
man revolted at further prostitution of his ecclesi-
astical powers. Wolsey was paid by the temporal
king whom he had served; he would not be paid by
the King of Eternity whom he had not served.

The national hero, even when truly heroic, is
forsaken by the people when the national mind is
defiled by insidious propaganda. Being truly heroic,
he continues to worship and to obey the realities.
He has not courted the fictitious; therefore repudia-
tion by the fictitious does not alter his trend. The
genius of life supports him; that is his predestined
reward. The charlatan has his reward in the brief
applause of the public. What the fictitious promotes

it also overthrows. Like produces like; like seeks and inevitably finds like; like cleaves to like and coalesces with like in all realms, world without end. A high seat in the synagogue is reserved for you if you are living on the level of its altitude.

To get, you must give. The metaphysician did not make this law; he discovered it. When you understand this law you will acknowledge it to be the loveliest provision in the Mind of God. With a delight hitherto unknown, you will delight in knowing this law and in keeping it with utmost fidelity in every detail. The law is your agent that exchanges the fictitious for the real in your mind.

If you try to get without giving you will get a hard heart; you will feel that you must be served without regard to the welfare of others. If you try to get without rendering an equivalent for what you obtain you will get a misunderstanding of life. There must be displacement or there is no room for the new, no room for expansion of that which you would increase. If you try to get without sharing you will be forced to present a petition in bankruptcy before the court of life; you will not have given and received for the benefit of all those necessarily interested in the transaction.

Life is exchange between you and God. You name what is exchanged and how much is exchanged. Give your limited good for His unlimited good. Give your foolishness for His wisdom. Give your weakness for His strength. The fictions that you offer Him will cease in His realities, to trouble you and the universe no more.

Challenge God to a race in giving and see if you can disburse more rapidly and more fully than He will reimburse. If possible to conceive, let your ideal be that of giving more than you get, thus showing yourself to be opulent, fearless, magnificent. When you give you are rich—you have enough to share. When you do not give you are poor—you have little for yourself, and that little will diminish under the unwise treatment of hoarding. By continued inactivity the germ in the acorn shrinks; becomes incapable of growth; finally it dies.

You receive what you give. Have you ever quarreled? If you have, you can recall how you received what you gave: Bitter words, sharp retorts, in hard tones and accompanied by angry looks, catapulted forth and volleyed back. That was a giving intended to burden the receiver with shame; that was a receiving that scorched and abashed. Have you ever spoken the word of sincere esteem? Corresponding to the sentiment, your tone softened, your eyes were eloquent of good will. Then, also, you received as you gave, respect for respect, appreciation for appreciation. Life is just, exact. If you still are a baby in mind, you will fear that fact. If you are feeding your mind on the food that promotes growth, you will welcome that fact as an opportunity to prove your mettle.

You benefit by what you bestow, if you have learned life well enough to know that you cannot be deprived of reality. All truth is susceptible of proof in the exoteric as in the esoteric. Immunity from the pains of the exoteric is gained by conscious habitation in the esoteric. The need for physical sustenance was satisfied in Jesus by His giving the water of life to the woman at the well. Joan of Arc warned her executioners to stand away from the fire that was consuming her body. Such occurrences as these are not of the supernatural; they are of the superhuman. They are of the real world; you have the support of the realm in which you consciously live. The senses make no demand on the spiritual consciousness, in which you have eternal life and never-failing sustenance. I have proved this to a degree, and in this particular manner:

At one time I lived in a district where the water was unpleasingly flavored by mineral solutions. Consequently the water to be used as drink was filtered.

One evening at a social affair I became thirsty. I spoke of wanting a drink. The woman with whom I had been talking also wanted a drink. We went into the refreshment room. Neither of us cared for fruit punch; we both asked for water.

Only a half glass of filtered water was available. The attendant proffered me the water. I took the glass and held it out to my companion, asking her to drink. She demurred, but I insisted. Finally I said, "I am sure that if you will drink the water I shall cease to be thirsty." She looked mystified. Again I urged her, and she drank. When she had drained the glass my thirst ceased. For the remainder of the evening I was as thoroughly refreshed as I would have been had I drunk all the water that I at first felt I needed. I do not remember drinking on reaching my home.

You possess what you give. What you bestow on another is his; it still is yours, because you have in you the consciousness of the thing. To be conscious of a thing is to possess it. Consciousness is the germ of things, and you possess whatever you impart; your giving opens in you the floodgates to the exhaustless resource. If you will remember that truth you never will feel depleted.

What you share you increase. "If two of you shall agree on earth as touching anything that they shall ask, it shall be done for them of my Father who is in heaven." In whatever you agree with the sons of God, you share with them. In whatever you agree with another to ask of God, you receive, and the other receives. Two of you become conscious of possessing where before neither was conscious of possessing. You retain what you impart: You have a garden of lovely roses. I look at your garden, and say, "Your roses are wonderfully fair." You select the loveliest rose, cut it from the stem, and present it to me. Though I bear the rose away with me, it still is your rose. Your love, your attentive watchfulness, your devotion to beauty, produced the rose. What you produce is yours. What you give me is mine. You have your loveliest rose; I have your loveliest rose. Nothing can take the rose from me to whom you gave the rose. Nothing can take the rose from you while you retain the spirit of the rose. There was one rose; your giving has made it become two roses.

Life is just, exact. God is merciful, the opulent bestower of Himself. Amen.

Heard are the voices,
  Heard are the sages,
  The world and the ages:
Choose well; your choice
Is brief, and yet endless.

Here eyes do regard you
  In eternity's stillness;
  Here is all fullness,
Ye brave, to reward you:
Work, and despair not.

You are the justly recompensed worker of the universe.

Life pays. It pays me all that I am worth.
I give as I receive. I receive as I give.
I give myself to God that I may receive Him.

YOUR OBJECTIVE
Chapter 6

When the captain of a mighty ocean liner clears from port and turns the prow of his vessel into the sea lane indicated by chart and compass, he knows what his objective is. By all his innate knowledge, by all the skill of his seamanship, by all the manhood that is in him, he sets himself to bring his vessel safely to the haven of his promise. He circumvents or uses tides and weather; he directs his crew; he controls the mechanism of his craft; he adapts to his needs all agencies and all circumstances that will contribute to his delivery of his precious cargo at the port of destination. You would not fear to commit your body, your credentials, and your wealth to the care of that captain. He knows where he is going; his objective is definite, understandable. He does not guess, nor does he particularly hope. He knows, and he does.

The captain of a tramp vessel drives from port to port, swerving with the trend of trade as he picks up a cargo. His objective changes. After years of cruising, he may bring his craft to the port you seek. But you would not ship with him on the probability of his touching that port. You take passage on the vessel that drives direct to the shore that commands your interest.

The battered derelict that rolls to passing swells, that yields to winds and tides, that lags in sargassos or lurches helplessly in the drift and turmoil of a typhoon, has no objective. You would not trust your life and your fortune to such a vessel as that.

The ship of the dead viking, floating ablaze, has a destination—the ocean floor. It is a ship of death; oblivion in the unknown deeps is its objective. You would not take passage on that ship and let yourself be cut away from the land of the living.

The objective is the most important consideration in life. There is no definite place in life for you while you keep your mind purposeless. If you live merely because you are alive, for you there will be no quickening of the pulses, prophetical of stronger living. For you there will be no eager intake of breath in the morning, as you have nothing but hours before you. For you there will be no grateful outgo of breath in the evening, as you have not accomplished that which commands content. The magnificent unrest, the goading joy, the tingle that comes of matching adequacy with need, will be yours when you choose a work, swear before high heaven to *do* that work, and then in the strength of heaven set about *doing*.

Have you an objective? Have you chosen your port of destination? What do you hope to make of yourself? Do you know what you want to do? Have you a conception of what you are accomplishing?

Your objective is what you supremely wish to do; what you most ardently wish to become; what, with the utmost passion of your soul, you endeavor to achieve within yourself.

If you have not already determined your objective, consult life's possibilities and make your choice. Decide what objective you will have. If you resolve to do your present work perfectly, or if you choose a new line of endeavor, at the moment of making your decision begin to bend all your energies to the attainment of your objectives. If what you choose now is God's eternal now, it will forever abide, and your work for it will eternally prosper you. If what you choose is of the time world you will tire of it or it will fail you. Then you will be compelled to forego that objective and to select another. Pray God now for intelligence now to choose what will last, and what will increasingly bless and enrich you.

The illusory objectives of the fictitious world have their culmination in power over human kind. The soul is sensible of power, whatever its circumstances. But not until it knows itself spiritually does it understand that its power is to be devoted only to the work of setting itself right with life. The agency of power in the fictitious world is some form of political dominance or some form of financial supremacy. And, to avoid what might be construed as the snub of silence, mention might be made of the teaching that you can have as an objective the power of mental control of others.

The use of any power by which you bend others to your will is destructive to your best aims and to your freedom. If you control others you become responsible for their acts, and for their very lives. Moreover, your interference reacts in dissatisfaction on your part, and ultimately you find yourself disappointed, unhappy. You learn by experience, if you are too headstrong to learn from observation and too unresponsive to heed the teachings of innate wisdom, that you cannot prosper while you violate the sacred right of initiative in others.

Alexander of Macedon selected world power as his objective. Upon being informed that an infinite number of worlds existed, he wept "because we have not yet conquered one." His objective excluded the real values of life. He wept not with the orphans whose fathers had fallen to give him power. He wept not with the widows whose husbands had been sacrificed to insure him supremacy. He wept not for the devastation of fair places and the destruction of men's work. He has been called Alexander the Great. He was greatly destructive, greatly murderous, but not greatly a great man. His objective inhibited the activity of the greatness that is real, the greatness that induces content. Disappointed, unhappy, this king who had greatly abused his great opportunity to serve, closed his time life with a span of thirty-three years.

Mind knows that initial act is the beginning of result; mind knows that the act cannot be separated from its effect. So legend, tradition, myth, fancy, and fairy tale support history in emphasis of the truth that, when attained, the selfish objective rewards the seeker with discontent. Joy to the unselfish, sorrow to the selfish, is the apportionment. King Midas prayed that he might be given the golden touch. As all prayer is answered King Midas was given the power whereby the objects that he touched were turned to gold. This was a foolish

prayer, and one obviously destined to be most awk-
ward in fulfillment. But Midas, in the sentiment, if
not in the language of modernism, wanted what he
wanted—and received what he asked. His selfish
prayer plagued and grieved him when it began to
work. Midas had to pray again, "even as you and
I," for the reversal of the prayer that was conceived
in ignorance, made in selfishness, and found insup-
portable in fruition.

The control of others by means of silent suggestion is an objective that presents itself only to
meager minds of ambitious tendencies. One who has
even a rudimentary sense of honesty does not consider such a use of power. One who has any regard
for the sanctity of the soul does not choose an objective so profane. One who respects his own integrity does not attempt to violate the integrity of
another. Whatever plausibilities of "success" may
be presented as justification for the practice, the
fact remains that its devotees do secretly what they
would not dare to do openly. The secrecy imposed
avows the character of the work. The practice of
suggestion is referred to in the Gospels as a thief
who, before despoiling the house, binds the strong
man who should protect the house.

The thief never enters the house whose strong
man knows himself to be a son of God. You never
will be touched by direct or by indirect suggestion
after you have regained your spiritual consciousness.
The bonds that the thief would fasten on you are
as ropes of water that spill out of his hand. You
remain unfettered.

No one can influence you by suggestion without your consent. Fear is a form of consent. Acknowledgment of power renders you susceptible to the power that you acknowledge. What you think that you can do to another you will think that another can do to you. The cleansing that frees your mind from the secret ambition to control others also cleanses you of the fear that others can control you.

The Mind of God flows outward as your mind. It bears defilements from you and dissolves them as it carries them away. Cast into that stream both your faith and your fear that suggestion can compel you. Then the uncleanness of suggestion will depart from you.

Attempt to influence by silent suggestion is the work of a Frankenstein who assembles dead things and makes of them a monster that destroys its author. When you understand what you are you will respect yourself in a way that will prevent your entering into this practice. When you understand what life is you also will understand that the "monster" cannot be made to attack any but its creator. Then self-preservation will forbid your use of silent suggestion.

Attempted control of another through silent suggestion bears no resemblance to the act of praying for the welfare of another. The welfare of the one for whom you pray is secured in his finding freedom in God. It does not come for your gratification at seeing manifest what you may think is needed. Any improvement that comes to another does not warrant your celebrating yourself. You never did

and never can heal anyone. You never did and you
never can prosper anyone. You never did and never
can do more for anyone than to refrain from med-
dling with his life.

There is an objective that embraces all your
good. That objective is service.

Working for this objective, you awaken. As
you near this objective you feel the nature of God
stirring in you. When you have passed all that at
one time lay between you and this objective, you
find that you have become conscious of aliveness.
You then know why God must give all of Himself
for the mere asking. Jesus, who had dominion
over life and earth and heaven, said of Himself,
"The Son of man came not to be ministered unto,
but to minister." Power in life, in earth, and in
heaven, lies in ability to minister. Service is co-ordina-
tion with the laws of being. It is the law of heaven.

When you see others working with apparent
ease and much success you may feel that you are
not progressing as rapidly as you should. The comparison between your work and their work is based
on your ignorance of the effort and the consecration
that they have made to induce the facility that you
admire. If you will try with all the industry of which
you are capable, you will find yourself nearing your
objective. You may say, "If I could teach as my
favorite teacher teaches, and if I could write as my
favorite writer writes, how happy I should be!" Do
you think that your teacher and your writer attained
their present states of proficiency by merely wishing
to do the work that they are doing? Be assured that

the excellence which you admire and should like to parallel has come through work: development of consciousness and the application of consciousness.

Work, if you would grow into your ideal. "No man becomes a saint in his sleep." All seasons are yours. While you are awake your mind appropriates, gathers the food that makes it grow. While you are asleep your mind assimilates what you have fed it. The objective fades if it is not pursued. Then, until you select another objective, or until you rechoose your first objective and work for your choice, there is an apparent pause in your development.

All things in the marts of life are bought at par value. There are no bargain counters at the place of exchange where God gives Himself to you in the precise measure of your giving yourself to Him. Having chosen your objective, are you willing to pay the price of the prize?

The price is the devotion of your courage, your ability, your time, your very blood. The price is you. If you have purpose, if you have spirit, if you feel yourself to be alive, you will pay; will pay gladly, and thank God for the opportunity of receiving at any rate of exchange.

To prove that you are not seeking favors and that you are willing to earn what you ask, you will have to be steadfast, despite all obstacles that you may encounter. If you believe in yourself and in your objective, you will be given proof that opposition is nothing more than a phantom of the fictitious world. None of God's realities opposes you. All the powers and all the agencies of the kingdom of God are arrayed to encourage and to aid you. When you win your objective it is no longer a goal; it has become a part of you. It lends itself to the formation of a yet lovelier objective.

You cannot borrow your ideal. The perfections of God are epitomized in you. "Thy ideal is in thyself; thy impediment, too, is in thyself." If you will make the ideal your companion your impediment will be forgotten, and finally obliterated through lack of husbanding. Ideals are evolved, are attained. Then they take their places in your mental background; there they become a host to support you and to give you confidence.

If you inexpressibly yearn for the attainment of your ideal, if you want it more than you want anything else in life, you will push forward in the spirit of Paul, "But one thing *I do* . . . I press on toward the goal." Wanting it enough to make you try enough, you will reach your goal. Let that assurance keep you in good heart.

Permit nothing to come between you and your purpose. If your present objective does not compel your firmest allegiance and command the fullest of your admiration, pursue it no longer. You have all of God's eternity in which to achieve, but you have no minute of time to devote to the second best thing. Choose again. Choose what is dearest, fairest, most valuable of all things to you. Then let no argument prevail against your loyalty and your endeavor. Not the pattern shown in the mount to another, but the pattern there shown to you, is your objective. Do not be flattered or argued into accepting what is contrary to that which has been given you. Say with stanch old Luther, "Here I stand; I can no otherwise, so help me God."

If you let minor interests draw your attention from your main work you cannot rapidly prosper in your quest. When a farmer wants a bumper crop of corn he does not spend much time in his potato lot during the season of corn cultivation. He gives his time to his cornfield. The teacher and the writer whose abilities you admire did not and do not give their nights to amusements and their days to resting from amusements that they again at night may be amused. They followed along the path to their objective; they still follow. In season and out of season, through good report and ill, you also will follow the path if you do fully believe the thing that you think you have chosen as the Mecca of your heart.

The ideal always keeps a little in advance of you. As your vision clarifies you will see that the improvement which you first dreamed of making was but the initial step toward the goal. Your guiding star is not a stationary one. Having gained the eminence from which the light first shone, you find that the beacon has moved to higher ground. Pursue it rejoicingly, a song on your lips, courage in your heart. All the ground that you gain is good ground. If you weary, plod on. If you stumble, regain your march tread. If you are refreshed, speed forward. Always far enough ahead to keep you climbing, always near enough to give you comfort, up, and ever up, proceeds the beacon light. It is leading you along the hills of God to the summit of

His consciousness. Realities urge you forward. Fictions have no force to delay you. All things are possible. If you hold to your purpose, you will accomplish all that you attempt.

> Rest is not quitting
>   The busy career;
> Rest is the fitting
>   Of self to its sphere.
>
> 'Tis the brook's motion,
>   Clear, without strife
> Fleeing to ocean,
>   After its life.
>
> 'Tis loving and serving
>   The highest and best;
> 'Tis onward, unswerving—
>   This, this is true rest.

To attain your objective you do not have to compete with others. Competition belongs to the fictitious world, wherein it is felt that success is to him who outstrips all others. In the real world your aim is not to win at the expense of others, but to win at the expense of that part of you which still may cling to the fictitious. To compete is to employ the petty; to abstain from comparisons is to wing yourself with omnipotence. Your race is with yourself. You are to outstrip yourself. You, as conscious national of the real world, compete with you as victim of amnesia, wandering lost in the realm of the fictitious. This is the only form of competition permissible to you. Your objective includes the finding within yourself of the perfection that you dimly have sensed and gropingly have reached for in others, in circumstances, in outer attainment.

Everything that you have sought in the outer has reposed within you from the beginning of time. "Lord, show us the Father, and it sufficeth us," said Philip. When Philip transferred consciousness from eternity to time, he forgot the look of God and the place of His abode. With mind distracted by the events of time, the Cause temporarily is lost to sight. Though the Cause repose, you are in unrest. Faint stirrings of memory trouble you—and give you hope. You would see, you would hear, you would touch the Cause, which is too near to you for you to contact through the senses. "I am in the Father, and the Father in me." There is no excellence, no bliss for you outside yourself. Reality is within.

You move from experience to experience in time; you pass from consciousness to consciousness in eternity. You always are to understand that in speaking of time you are considering events. Time is not the place of the living; it is the field of experience. In speaking of eternity you consider causes. Eternity is not the place of the dead. It is the place of the living. In eternity all things abide. In time all things change; event succeeds event. Failure is no part of life. A state of consciousness is as definite as the results that it produces. If you begin something while in one state of consciousness and enter another state of consciousness before that thing is finished, you cannot have a complete product of the first state. If you begin a thing in high en-

thusiasm and finish in a ragged funk you will not
have a perfect product. But this is not failure. You
carry the products as far as you carry your consciousness in that respect. You succeed so far as you maintain the cause of success. Never say that you have
failed. You may have ceased to try, and so did not
complete the matter that you began. It is quite impossible that you should fail, but it is quite possible
that you may desert a work before you have finished
it. If you wish to bring to a perfect consummation a
thing that you now have in hand, do not let go of it
by switching from your present consciousness regarding it to another consciousness regarding it.

There is no defeat. There may be postponement.
If you surrender to fear; if you think that there are
insurmountable impediments, and so cease to try,
your work comes to a standstill. If the owner of a
factory suspends operations, some articles of his
manufacture may be left in a state of partial com-
pletion. But that is not defeat. When the owner
again sets his machinery into productive activity he
will finish what was left unfinished. If he abandons
his former line of product for a new line, he is not
defeated, nor has he failed. He has changed his
objective. He will succeed in his new line if he has
intelligence, courage, and perseverance.

You have intelligence. You are intelligent because
God's intelligent mind operates your mind. You have
courage because you know what is backing you. You
have perseverance because you know that you produce, all the time, and that you can produce what
you choose to produce. So you cannot be defeated.

If postponements occur you know what causes them. Fortune, chance, results, all proceed from you.

The present is an area in life too small to contain the ultimate of your endeavors. It is too small to give you a true perspective of what you are accomplishing. Each day brings a partial result, and today's partial result is carried forward, daily. You are not willing to wait for your outer success, your vindication? The Nazarene Carpenter has waited almost two thousand years, and still waits. Do not be impatient with time; do not despair of increasing success and of final complete triumph. In a onetime-present area they said of Jesus, "He saved others; himself he cannot save." Time-blind were they, to think that eternity's cause could be accurately presented in a day. That which on the first Black Friday was pronounced a loss was the beginning of an infinite salvation. If you do the real thing that you undertake to do, despite judgments, scourgings, and Golgothas, you too will serve the divine objective: not to be ministered unto, but to minister.

If you say that His cause was so great, so high, so divine that in itself it contained unfailing inspiration and support; that your cause is commonplace and therefore subject to small annoyances and nagging smarts, you do not read from the book of life what I read. Jesus had His work; you have your work. For His work He was responsible to God; for your work you are responsible to God. His work met oppositions that never will be offered to yours, oppositions that never can be repeated on this planet: traps by lawyers, traps by theologians;

plots, lies, defamations, desertions, disloyalties, physical hurts, crucifixion of soul and body. His work
protects your work, insuring it and you from hurt.
You forget His time experiences in the honors that
have accrued to Him for the appointed work fulfilled
in both letter and spirit. You think only of His present exalted life and contrast with it your present
humble life. But to stop with that comparison is to
ignore the fact that you are an idea in the mind of
God, and therefore indispensable to the universe.
Your life will receive its meed of glory in its proper
sphere, if you reach your objective as He reached
His. Your responsibility has an extent as far-reaching as your consciousness. "To whomsoever much is
given, of him shall much be required." Aware of
your divine character, you are aware of your divine
responsibility. *Noblesse oblige.*

Victory first is achieved within yourself. The
abiding outer triumph is the tablet that records
your permanent triumphs over the phantoms of the
fictitious world. When you cease to regard oppositions as personal and recognize them as your response to the challenge of environment, you find
yourself able to ignore them. When you ignore them
you divest them of power to interfere with you.
Keep within your own sphere—the real world. There
you meet your own, respond to your own. The fictitious cannot pursue you there or confront you
there. "A gentleman will not insult me, and none
other can." Victory is in your accurate concept of
being: You know that you are an idea in the Mind
of God, and that you therefore are, as He is, love.

You do not war with anyone. You are the love that fulfills the law. You reach your objective because love cannot fail.

Victory is in your feeling: You know that your mind is the use that you make of the Mind of God. You perfectly react to the Mind of God, and you become aware of the power of God in you to understand and to do according to the specifications of the love that fulfills the law. You win your goal because the power of God cannot be thwarted.

Victory is in your living: You know that the substance of God is shaped by your use of it. Letting the Mind of God think you, malformations cannot appear in your life. Love and power unite to do their perfect work in you. Mind, body, environment, slough off the fictitious, and the real emerges. You attain your ideal because the ideal is the jewel in the setting of substance. It is the image-Likeness of God in you.

Now is the beginning. Here is the place. Not waiting until you are wiser, but beginning now to use wisdom; not hoping to develop the strength necessary for the conquest, but developing strength by using strength, so shall you without delay draw near to your objective. Not looking afar, but searching here; not groping toward the unknown, but in the place called present environment, lay hold of your ideal. The ideal begotten of the Father is Jesus Christ. The ideal begotten of Jesus Christ is life, perfect within and perfect without. Concerning beginnings, the Father said of His ideal, "This day have I begotten thee." Of continuation that embraces

place, Jesus said, "I am with you always." The ideal
and the way to the ideal are now present, now
unmistakable.

> You will be what you will to be;
> Let failure find its false content
> In that poor word "environment."
> But spirit scorns it, and is free.

The supreme power with which you are co-
operating never is defeated. Your supreme objective
is to let that power function in you.

Any objective is attainable. Only the supreme
objective is worthy of your aspiration and endeavor.
All objectives less glorious than the supreme objective will dim, cease. The night of forgetfulness
will pass. There will dawn in your consciousness
the glory of that perfection which never deserted
you, which waited while you wasted, which called
while you slept. To grasp that glory in mind, in soul,
and in body; to have and to hold its beauty and its
peace, will become your final objective. To the attainment of this objective God pledges you His aid,
His comfort, and His eternity.

You are the seeker who finds.

My objective is to find myself.

My objective is to understand life.

My objective is to know God.

God is my inspiration, my way, my strength.
He brings me to Himself.

YOUR EQUIPMENT
Chapter 7

When a carpenter goes forth in the morning to begin his day's work, he goes supplied with an equipment of the tools that are required by his trade. He puts each tool to its intended use in his line of work. With saw and hammer and square, he does not try to lay a brick wall or to shoe a horse.

When an artist assembles color tubes, brushes, palette, and canvas, he does so for the purpose of painting a picture. With the tools of his trade, he does not attempt to reduce a block of marble to the exquisite proportions of a Madonna or to the heroic outlines of a Hercules.

The worker reveals his trade by the kind of tools that he uses. The singer uses his voice; the athlete uses his body; the weaver uses his loom. The product of the worker reveals the skill with which the tools have been employed. A mediocre product is the sign of a mediocre worker; a superior product is the sign of a worker who has some advantage over the one whose product is mediocre.

The advantage possessed by the superior worker rarely is to be called a natural gift. Usually it is a development. The superior worker uses all his equipment, and he steadily increases his equipment. To improve himself and his work is his great objective, and to the attainment of his objective, he directs all his resources. The mediocre worker lacks an inspiriting objective. He is not outstandingly eager to improve himself or his product.

If you are a superior worker you know that you can win, and you make yourself win. If you are a mediocre worker you will neglect to take with you to your daily occupation the most necessary of all tools—confident aspiration. You become discontented, chronically unsuccessful; you set your success in the future and there it remains. You claim that your troubles are due to injustice somewhere. You say that economic inequalities forbid your success. You think that the remedy for your trouble lies in the acts of others; you are convinced that legislation can do for you what you have not done for yourself.

Social customs and legislated laws are the expressions of the mental and the moral development of the people in the areas where the customs and the laws operate. If you demand that changes be made in the unwritten and in the written laws that operate in your area, begin the changes by making changes in yourself. In doing this you will create an unvoiced, but nevertheless a definite call for those laws. Make yourself a beneficiary of the better laws, even before they are created. Justice is not dead, not asleep, not on vacation. The better customs and laws that you wish to see in operation will begin to act at the moment of humanity's readiness for them. Governments are as good and as just as are warranted by the intelligence and the consciousness of the people governed. Your thought, your life, your work, contribute to the demand that foreruns social and economic changes. Stop knocking and go to nailing, if you would have a better community and a better national structure. You have active influence in all the spheres of life.

You are equipped to meet the demands of every sphere that you enter. If you have not been meeting the demands of your sphere, begin now to use the equipment that will adjust you and your sphere to each other. "A poor workman blames his tools." If you have been a poor workman, discontented and apparently unsuccessful, the condition is in part due to your having tried to paint your masterpiece on canvas with a chisel—an instrument that you should reserve for your work in marble. No doubt the chisel is a good chisel; it will lend itself to good work in its proper medium. When you apply it to another medium you do not have pride in the result. Fit your equipment to your work, and you will not blame your tools. You will be pleased with the result.

You came into this world equipped to meet every demand that this world will make of you.

You have a brain. Use it. You acquired it for use. Your brain is solely for your use; it is the only brain in the world whose work can be of particular value to you. Think; do not be content in playing at thinking. Your brain will enjoy the exercise involved in real thinking; dormant cells will awake, and all awake cells will work for you. Search. Delve into the matter that interests you; do not be satisfied with skimming the surface. Then knowledge, understanding, enjoyment, will reward your efforts. Resolve every point that arises in any case. Use your full mental equipment; you will progressively become a better worker.

You have a body. Train it to serve you, not to rule you. Educate it to health, strength, endurance. It provides contact with the visible world; therefore by all the improvement that you make in it you are the better served by it. Always keep your mind and your body in correct relationship: mind, the director; body, the agent.

You have an environment. Fill it with God. Never put into your environment anything that can hamper your most accurate expression of the God idea. You have to associate with and to do business with the ideas, the thoughts, the fancies that you give shelter in your consciousness. People your consciousness with good and your environment with good; then there will be no terrors for you to face, no jangled nerves to impair your ability. Then you and success will become a sturdy team, the universe looking on and cheering, the while.

The world is your field. Wherever mankind exists, there you exist. Wherever mankind hopes and tries, there you hope and try. You diffuse yourself through humanity; what you are makes itself felt, even though who you are remains unrecognized. Your equipment of brain, body, environment, is augmented by your ability, your training, and the practice that you have had. All these advantages brought to play in your field make of you a master worker.

The discipline that you give your mind, the information that you collect, will serve you in special needs. Years prior to the outbreak of the War between the States, the questions involved in that struggle engrossed the attention of the people. Fervid discourses, lofty appeals, acrimonious debates, demanded national audition. Prejudiced views and dispassionate considerations were offered. The climax of argument occurred in the Congress when Webster delivered his reply to the speech of Hayne. In the congratulations tendered Webster following the address, one admirer referred to the speech as a triumph of extemporaneous eloquence. Webster said that the speech was not extemporaneous; that he had known from the day when the preceding session closed that reassembling would bring forward the unsettled questions; that in the days of his intervening vacation he had been amassing the facts and the arguments that he had just delivered—to the great admiration of his sympathizers.

The presentation of your theme is based on preceding consideration of the theme. Perhaps the most truly extemporaneous speech ever made in this world was made by Adam during the famous interview in the garden. At that, Adam had to do some quick thinking against the background of consequences.

Every thought on any topic and every moment's consideration of any subject are preparations that enable you to speak, to speak tellingly. They form a mental equipment the mere possession of which gives you happiness.

Until you have become acquainted with your soul you cannot know what riches lie concealed beneath the exterior. Uncivilized tribes range a vast tract of virgin soil, seeking pasturage for their flocks. They may superficially cultivate the soil with a flint

or with a crooked stick. Under this cultivation they
raise sparse crops of cereal, which, supported by
nature's offering of fruit and berry and nut, make
frugal sustenance for their numbers. The civilized
man comes, observes the soil, and says, "This will
produce abundantly." He employs the modern engines of agriculture; he plows and mellows and
plants acres in a day; he cultivates his crops; he
stores in granaries, and he ships. Where the ignorant tribesman lives scantily, he lives opulently. He
knew what wealth lay in the soil, unused, until
knowledge made that wealth available.

A mineralogist observes the soil that is being
excavated by men who know nothing of mineralogy.
He sees thrown out a clay that is significant to him.
He says, "Diamonds should be found here." He sets
a force at work to expose the promising stratum.
The clay is closely inspected; clods are broken open,
and the diamonds that have lain concealed for ages
reward the man who knew where they were and how
to bring them to the surface.

A stream having origin in a mountain height
leaps in snowy foam and pearly spray and glint-
ing waterfalls down the precipitous slopes. The
aborigine camped by the stream, his evening fire jet-
ting fugitive lances of light into the greenery about.
The pioneer succeeded the aborigine, and a log cabin
was reared in the valley at the place where the mad-
cap waters compose themselves into a stately river.
The pioneer lighted his abode by a strip of cloth
fed with grease, or he used candles of his own making. Later, the triumph of the kerosene lamp gave

comparative brilliancy to the cabin's interior. But came a man who understood somewhat of nature's ways and her hidden arsenals of power. He hitched certain appliances to the rioting waters, and thereby transmitted a light as of numberless shining drops. A thousand dwellings drive forth night, and machinery spins in response to the conjunction of appliance and stream. The possibility had been there from the first day of the stream's descent of the mountain, but not until intelligence was brought to bear on the situation did the stream yield its magnificent contribution to the happiness and the well-being of humanity.

Life is the virgin soil. Within you are gifts, treasures, abilities. These you may find and enjoy. But you will have to bring them into the realm where they can be of service. To make your mind yield in the abundance that will nourish and enrich you, you will have to cultivate it. You will have to delve below the surface of appearances for the treasures of life; you will have to separate the jewel from its enshrouding clay. You will have to harness the energy that now dissipates itself aimlessly, and transform it into motive power and illumination. Your equipment in detail is the mechanism of heaven in aggregate. If you do not apply your equipment it remains of no value to you.

That use increases your equipment is obvious in experience. The rasping notes that a child draws in his first touch of the violin may be toned to melody and even mastery, as practice gives the child familiarity and assurance. A young woman in train-

ing for secretarial work confuses her stenographic
symbols, stumbles in trying to read them, and
clumsily operates her typewriter. By diligent practice
she converts these inefficiencies into perfection of
service. The spirit of success is compounded of
courage and effort. Postponement of realization is
the inevitable result of self-distrust and spasmodic
activity.

Nowhere else in the language of man is there
given such a lesson on use and nonuse as Jesus
taught in the parable of the pounds.

True in the smallest detail and true in the grand
totality, the man who used his pound and increased
it by ten pounds was made ruler over ten cities; the
man who with one pound gained five pounds more
was made ruler over five cities; the man who made
no use of his pound was deprived of his pound,
which was given to the man who had made the larg-
est gain. Jesus did not present this parable as an
exposition of divine reward or of divine retribution.
He was teaching that life is exact. Plant a tree in
good soil, give the tree water and air and sunlight,
and the tree will grow. Plant a tree in the rocky floor
of a dark, dry cave, and the tree will not grow. Use
causes increase; nonuse causes decrease. "Unto every
one that hath shall be given; but from him that
hath not, even that which he hath shall be taken
away from him."

Similarities find each other. Where one robin
goes in the spring other robins follow. Two drops
of water rush toward each other; they embrace; they
are merged, and each drop finds itself increased

by the size of the other. Justly, beautifully, exactly, naturally, "unto every one that hath shall be given." You have your pound; use it, and you will receive five pounds more, ten pounds more. Life owes you nothing; life never will owe you anything. The use of your equipment increases your equipment in every intended operation to which you put it. By that increase life keeps you recompensed.

Your ability is equipment. You have apparent ability and nonapparent ability.

Your apparent ability is the ability that you have developed. Your nonapparent ability is the ability that now is dormant in you; you can rouse this ability and set it to work for you.

You have all the ability that you can use; you have very much more ability than you ever have used. Your nonapparent ability is the genius of God, with which you as yet have not made intelligent union. The genius of God, operating variously, produces all phenomena. What you have developed of it is an infinitely small fraction of what you may develop.

Of the glories that lie in the deeps of God, Paul quoted, "Eye hath not seen, nor ear heard, neither have entered into the heart of man, the things which God hath prepared for them that love him."

King of the land, king of the sea, king of the air, man has yet one domain in which to establish his authority. That domain is his mind. Voice circling the planet, inventions proclaiming him a near-god, man has yet to put that control on his desires that will cause the lesser to serve the greater. The discoveries, the inventions, the sciences that man has brought into the world are some of the things that Paul included in his cryptic inventory. At about the middle of the nineteenth century, a man associated with the patent office of this country advised the discontinuance of that department of government because he believed that inventive genius had probed nature's last mechanical secret. The man was as wise, as foreseeing, as are those who today believe that there is an end to the resources of God or that novelty is exhausted.

Paul said that the things are prepared for those who love God.

This specification is well made. Love embodies confidence; it reaches forth to the thing loved. To be confident of unrevealed truths, facts, possibilities, is to invite their confidence in you and their reciprocal reaching toward you. Love and confidence are two items that you must be sure to include with the rest of your equipment.

Jesus preceded Paul in the teaching that there are hidden treasures and undeveloped gifts in you. In speaking of the Comforter to come, and in enumerating what the Comforter would bring, Jesus said, "I have yet many things to say unto you, but ye cannot bear them now." You possess unsuspected faculties; within your mental possibilities are unsuspected areas of consciousness; God, loving you, holds at your ability to receive, unsuspected forms of good. Always gaining the new, you are apprised of yet other newness alluringly agitating the curtains of ignorance behind which it awaits you; always the urge of the unrevealed to win you from staleness and apathy; always God your objective, you always find God to be the equipment that insures your success. Thus, the way to your objective; thus, the unrolling tapestry of life's endeavors, tersely called evolution.

When ability is greatly in evidence you will hear it spoken of as natural ability. All ability is natural ability; an artificial ability would be an impossibility. There may be pretense at ability, but the pretense is easily detectable; it does not produce the results that follow the exercise of ability. All ability is natural to you. Whatever you develop has its source in you; the development is due to your treatment of the source. The genius of God is under the command of your choice. You are equipped with the omniscience and the omnipotence of God. Compare that equipment with the equipment that you daily employ. The comparison will account for the results that have been unsatisfactory to you.

Willingness is the open door to advancement.

You must be willing to co-operate with your associates. If at times this is not easy for you to do, act as if you were willing. Doing this, you will find matters proceeding so smoothly that you will become willing to co-operate. You cannot win by withholding the contribution of your good will and your ability. I have seen this proved in a number of instances. One instance:

Two lads were employed in the same department of a business concern. A vacancy was to occur in another department. Both lads aspired to the position

to be vacated, as the appointment would be a pro-
motion. One lad excelled in personal appearance,
popularity, and apparent ability; but in the absence
of his supervisors he neglected his work, and by mis-
chievous pranks put the department into an uproar.
The other lad worked under all circumstances; he
never discounted his ability by any sort of inattention. He received the appointment. The popular,
handsome, capable lad, to punish the concern that
had not promoted him despite his inattention to
duty, resigned, signed a contract that for a number
of years bound him to another work in which pro-
motion could not occur.

You must be willing to co-operate with situations.
Your progress on the path of evolution has brought
you to your present surroundings. Discontent magni-
fies the features of your environment that you choose
to resent. Your resentment temporarily halts your
progress; your equipment is not directed to the best
purposes, and you suffer for its misuse. These facts
I have seen illustrated many times. I give you a story
supportive of these statements. The one who had
the experience related it to me:

"I had a good job. I did my work well, and I
was well paid. But I began to think that I was too
good for my job. I grouched and quarreled with myself until I persuaded myself to resign. That was
months ago. I have not since been able to find work,
and my old position is closed to me.

"The bank in which I had deposited my savings
has failed. I now have neither work nor money. But
I have learned something. I put myself on the side

of failure, and failure did a thorough piece of work for me. Once I get another chance, just watch me hold on!"

Another chance came; his former position again was opened to him. He accepted gratefully, and he held on. He became willing to co-operate with situations, and his familiar situation received him back. He thought that he had failed; he had only postponed appreciation of his opportunity and the success that it made possible for him.

You must be willing to co-operate with life. When you co-operate with life, life co-operates with you. It equips you with substantial proof of its sustaining, renewing presence. Life never will desert you, and while you co-operate with life you do not desert it. There is sustenance in life for you, and also there are building processes that cause apparent lack to become satisfying fullness. The details of your co-operation are not questioned; the act of co-operation is all that life requires of you. Again I give you one out of many examples:

A young man ran from a burning house, his clothing in flames. As he ran he tore his blazing garments from his body. He staggered into a hospital. Immediately he was given the best of attention, but the physicians in charge said that he could not recover from the burns that had seared more than one half of his body surface.

In bed, bandaged, suffering, the young man began to sing. The attendants said that he was rallying before transition. He sang on. Then they said that the singing was an expression of delirium caused

by suffering. He continued to sing. It was then said
that his singing was an effect of medicines administered. Still the young man sang. He recovered. He
said, "When I ran from the house with my clothing
in flames, I determined to live. I knew that if I could
keep my thoughts on life and could keep singing,
I should live."

He co-operated with life, and life co-operated
with him.

The willing spirit is a challenge to God. He accepts the challenge, and He prevails against you in
the sense that whereas you give Him your littleness
He gives you His greatness.

If you apply your equipment grudgingly you
restrict your success. Cheerful application of all that
you have, all that you are, enlarges your success.

The most unhappy spectacle in God's universe
is the sullen worker, who works because he must
work, with eyes hard set against the glory that flows
from the heart of endeavor. If you say, "I work
simply because my bread depends on my day's
wages," you tarnish your equipment by base uses.
You are to work because you are part of the machinery of the universe. Your daily supply will be issued
to you, "for your heavenly Father knoweth that ye
have need of" bread and dress and shelter. In divine
reciprocity your supply is contemporaneous with your
effort; in divine sequence the spirit that you put into
your work is your requisition for supply. If you work
only for bread, bread is all that you will receive—
usually bread of a poor sort and malnutritious.

The happiest sight in God's universe is the responsive worker. Glad for opportunity to prove himself, eager to contribute of himself, mind and body and spirit blended as one pulsing mechanism of ability, he moves to the divine tempo: "My Father worketh . . . and I work." If you so work, bread will be yours and the joy of banquets in the halls of heaven; dress will be yours, the loveliness of well-wrought robes; houses will be yours, fairer and richer mansions successively throwing wide their doors to give you entrance. God is good. God is just. God is merciful.

Opportunity is everywhere, always. It awaits your appreciation and your use. You cannot escape from it. Earth, heaven, and hell are crammed with opportunity. Time clamors, importuning you to cope with its needs; imploring you to earn its rewards. Eternity mutely, serenely, discloses its vistas of endeavor and consequence. Life is opportunity. God is equipment. You choose and use, or you choose and neglect.

You must proceed with life. You have no alternative. You survive all change; you create, and your creations follow you along the path of life. Your field is where you are; your equipment is what you have made it. Your field ever will be where you are; your equipment ever will be what you make it. Your ideal forever remains within yourself. The German youth of romance, whose way to the land of his choice closed against him, said, "I will return to my field, and I will say, 'Here or nowhere is America.'"

Be not wont to despise your equipment and your place. Be not morose if the chosen thing eludes you. If it is yours it will seek you, even as you seek it. If it

is but a hint of what is yours, the fact that it represents is now seeking you; the fact and you will find
each other. What God has joined together not time
or space or even blundering can keep apart.

Here is all fullness, ye brave, to reward you;
Work, and despair not.

Within your present environment lies the glow-
ing paradise you seek. Here or nowhere is your
flawless equipment. Here or nowhere is opportunity.
Here or nowhere is God.

On an occasion of being commended for his
literary achievements, Richter said, "I have done
what I could with the stuff." Nothing unused of
his equipment, nothing neglected of his opportunity,
his product was testimony of his ability; it was his
offering to life, his impress of the genius of God.

"I have done what I could with the stuff." Trained
mind and body to serve the highest purposes in life;
used ability as an exercise to increase ability; will-
ingly co-operated with every essential contact; met
each opportunity with the superlative response.

Are you doing what you can with the stuff?

You are the worker who perfectly applies his
perfect equipment to each day's work.

My equipment is the genius of God.
My opportunity is here.
I will do what I can with the stuff.

YOUR RESOURCE
Chapter 8

A growing tree is rooted in the ground, from which it extracts nourishment. Secretly, industriously, the rootlets reach into untapped areas of soil, and therefrom draw the elements that, acted upon by the life force in the tree, prosper growth and fruitfulness. The alchemistic processes whereby mineral and air and water become a tree are beyond the scrutiny of human eyes. But that the processes occur, any one of your five senses may tell you. The tree is there; you even know the kind of tree it is. Not by the invisible roots do you know the nature of the tree, but by trunk and branch and leaf, by bud and blossom and fruit.

Your life has its roots in the invisible; its character is known by the appearance that it presents in the visible. Secretly, industriously, your life processes are carried on in the soil of mind. Thought rootlets reach into new areas where novel concepts and attractively rearranged old concepts are to be found. These are seized by the life force and are borne by the circulatory currents into the structure of your life. If the elements thus appropriated are of the highest nutritive value, renewed vitality, more symmetrical growth, and the germ of golden fruits are released in you.

Your life is in perpetual flower, fed by the vital essence contained in your thoughts. It is in perpetual fruit, the ripened forms of your thoughts. The transmutation of thought into flesh never is witnessed by the senses. That it takes place your changing life gives proof.

Had there been no mind to mold it, our universe would not have been formed. Chaos would have ruled throughout pulseless eternity. Were mind withdrawn from the manifest universe, that universe would crumble to elemental formlessness. Had there been no substance to mold, our manifest universe would have been impossible of organization. Mind would have held sway within itself, unproductive, monotonous. Were substance to be withdrawn, our manifest universe would vanish as light vanishes when the flame is extinguished.

To induce mental balance you must construct a consciousness that can deal with the absolute and remain practical, that can deal with the relative and not become materialistic. Occasionally to consider life in the absolute is refreshing; to do so washes the clay from your eyes and hushes the din of the time world. Wholly to discard the relative is to throw yourself out of step with the march of events; is to make you miss the cue for your next act. In your present development life is both absolute and relative. You must consider mind and you must consider substance, in which your mind works. Mind is your equipment in full; substance is the pliant stuff of your life. Contemplation of the absolute may defer physical demands, but it will not abolish physical demands. You are mind, but you have built a body that you must cherish.

You are absolute; for the present you are also relative. Mind must have a background against which to draw its pictures, a clay out of which to fashion its forms. Sufficient unto the day are the demands thereof. You will not finish with the relative until you have identified each phase of it with its origin, and merged it therewith. Substance in mass and substance in definite form are your two great considerations in the relative world. Your relation to substance in mass embodies power to determine the forms that substance assumes in your life. But you must know your tools and how to use them. The plutocrat and the beggar use tools identical in nature, but the product of the first is opulence while that of the second is penury.

Substance is the elemental quality of the food that produces growth and fruit in the tree. It is the elemental quality that feeds your body; that gave itself in the genesis of your body; that sustains and that lends itself to the re-creation of all organisms.

Substance is your resource, your support. It is your bodily support; it is your financial support. Substance is the element; support is the transmutation of substance into the diversified forms that daily minister to your physical life and its comforts. Bread, butter, potatoes, are not the elemental quality that is food. They are containers of the elements that through transmutations and distributions become food. They are conveyors of food; they bring from nature to your body the elements that you have taught your body to demand. Transmutation of the food element begins when the element is accepted by your mind. At the instant of the mind's approval the element is picked up by the life force and is car-

ried to the point of demand. During transportation
the element undergoes other changes. At the point
of demand it becomes liquid, tissue, bone, according to the need of your body when your body is in
normal condition.

A similar transmutation of substance fits it to
the needs of your life in areas not purely physical
but tributary to the physical. To work intelligently
with substance you must accept the fact that in all
matters of supply you deal with the element and
convert it to the form that fits your need. Bodily
support is maintained through intimate co-operation
of the life force in you and the food elements that
you give your body. These transactions involve hidden processes that you cover by the word "nature."
Your financial support is maintained by intimate
co-operation between the life force in you and the
substance element that manifests in the forms called
financial resource.

Your mind controls the life force in you. Whatever may have been your experience, you will find
that to treat the elemental substance as the immediate, quickly responsive resource, will prove to you
that substance is your financial resource as surely
as it is your physical resource.

In the absolute your support is direct from God,
who is the substance within matter, the element that
sustains eternal life. In literal fact your support is
God, but your obligations to the relative necessitate
the employment of forms. You cannot desert your
creation. You cannot outrage even your most foolish
mental images; you must transform them into images

that wear the glory of wisdom. Financial resource will continue to be a necessity until you learn how to receive life direct from God, and in so receiving possess the eternal base of financial resource.

Intelligent contact with substance is your most pertinent need in the visible world. The tree lives and grows by what we call unconscious use of substance. The use that you make of substance duplicates the use that the tree makes of substance until your mind begins to ask questions concerning the perpetuation of the body. The tree is not supposed to ask such questions. When the questions arise in your mind you and the tree part company in the matter of interest in substance, but not in the matter of the use of substance. When either you or the tree ceases to use substance in a way that would keep the body healthily sustained, disintegration begins. In either case, if the disintegrating process continues the body collapses.

Your practical interest in substance centers in its availability. There are four ways by which you may shut off the flow of substance in your life. If you check the flow of substance, destruction of your body, or financial entanglements, will ensue. Perhaps both will result. The four ways of shutting off the substance flow:

1. Treating substance as if it were decreasing in volume.

2. Treating substance as if it were fixed of form.

3. Treating substance as if it were insufficient to demand.

4. Treating substance as if it were restricted in agencies of distribution.

Political economists have mishandled the question of supply. Metaphysicians have taught only a portion of the law of supply. Through the delineation of miracles the Bible teaches the perfect law of supply, and also shows how the law may be ignored, to the decrease of supply. How the flow of supply is regulated is illustrated in four outstanding miracles. These illustrations specify the form of lack, then give the processes by which plenty supplants lack. The treatment of substance that insures supply embodies four points that counteract the movements that check supply. The points are:

1. Consideration of substance that recognizes it as steady of volume.

2. Consideration of substance that recognizes its adaptability.

3. Consideration of substance that recognizes its sufficiency in every case.

4. Consideration of substance that recognizes unrestricted agencies of distribution.

The four Biblical illustrations:

THE PROPHET AND SUPPLY: The Prophet Elijah brought drought on the land ruled by King Ahab.

After the drought had continued for some time Elijah was forced to move from his retreat by the brook Cherith. His prophecy was working smoothly; the stream had dried. Elijah's activities began to assume a resemblance to those of the dog, which, "to gain its private ends, *went* mad, and bit the man."

Taking advice of Jehovah, Elijah went to Zare-

phath. At the city gate he met the widow who was
to provide him food. Having drunk of his own
drought, the prophet was thirsty; he asked the
widow to bring him a drink. As the widow turned
to go for the water the prophet requested her to
bring him a little bread. The widow goes on record:
"As Jehovah thy God liveth, I have not a cake, but
a handful of meal in the jar, and a little oil in the
cruse: and, behold, I am gathering two sticks, that
I may go in and dress it for me and my son, that we
may eat it, and die."

The visible aspect of the situation has been out-
lined. Attention now should be transferred to the
mental acts that operated to originate and to complete the visible situation.

A spiritual prophet is one who delivers a divine
message. A practical prophet is one who uses his
power of mind to shape a specific result. In the case
under consideration, Elijah was a practical prophet.
He used his mental power to score against Ahab and
also to take care of himself. A widow is defined as
"a woman who has lost her husband by death and is
still unmarried." To widow means "to deprive of
something desirable, or that suggests a husband's
. . . support." The widow of Zarephath had been
widowed in a double sense: Her husband had died,
and by her penurious considerations of supply she
had deprived herself of what suggested a husband's
support. She had been believing that substance would
cease to support her, and by her mental shutting
down on substance she was lessening her store of
visible supply. Her treatment of substance had so

effectively prevailed on her supply that she considered two sticks sufficient to her culinary demands.

The life force is tenacious of its forms. It tries
to convince you that it needs your body as a mode of
expression. This fact is indicated by the terms that
you instinctively stipulate when prophesying dis-
aster on small or on large scale. You keep a back
door open, through which you hope to escape when
the avenger enters the front door. Elijah had his
brook, his raven; after that, the widow was to provide for him. The widow had her meager supply.
She expected that small supply to fail; but she did
not expect it to fail before she again availed herself
of its comforts. Starvation was only a little beyond,
but it was beyond. Persistent is the life force. The
widow postponed her dying by starvation. She would
have another square meal, or a meal as nearly square
as she could make it, before beginning to starve to
death.

The widow was ignorant in regard to the law
that regulates supply. The prophet knew the law. He
persuaded the widow to treat her little of meal and
her little of oil in the way that would make them
become as springs calling to the hidden streams of
plenty. Under this treatment the outflow continued.
The persons of the household were sustained.

On this miracle has been based the metaphysical teaching that you must share your supply if you
would insure continuation of your supply. This
teaching is correct in itself, but it is not the whole of
the teaching implied. Though you should invest in
the best of securities, and though you should share

to your last crust, you cannot make your supply steady until you treat it as being based on constant, essential substance.

Not essentially your possessions, but essentially your spirit toward your possessions, makes you rich or poor. When you give, let the gift be made in conjunction with the fact that substance cannot be diminished in volume. When you start supply into circulation, let it represent the pound that the thrifty servant used in gaining ten pounds of increase. If you feel that you cannot share you are poor in mind. Then, despite your external accumulations, some day you will know yourself to be a beggar, forever trying to receive, forever trying to withhold.

The widow learned that sharing precedes replenishment. She shared. She treated her supply as constant. Her supply became constant. The miracle of continuation, worked in the widow's meal and oil, presents two provisions of the law of supply:

1. Keep supply in circulation; send out.

2. Treat the inner elemental substance and the outer form of substance supply as continuous in nature. Expect replenishment.

If you have the courage to submit your interests to the provisions of the law that were observed in this miracle, you will prove for yourself that supply is constant.

You are more likely to forswear yourself in your intention toward supply than in any other way. You say that when you are prospered you will give liberally to worthy causes; you will be generous; you will not use your income selfishly, but will de-

vote it to good works. Then, when supply begins to
increase you find personal ways in which to apply
the increment. The house with which you thought
you would be content will be so much more desirable, so much more satisfactory, if its proposed un-
pretentious dimensions and interiors be enlarged and
embellished. The long dreamed of trip will be so
much more enjoyable if taken in a luxurious suite instead of in the modest accommodations that at one
time seemed acceptable to you. Your associations
change, and the changes are expensive. You must
keep up appearances; you must dress as richly as your
friends dress, must have as many and as good cars
as your friends have. Your tastes take on the qualities
suggested by your fortune; what had been luxuries
become necessities. Of the volume of supply that
you once thought would provide a surplus for unselfish expenditures no surplus remains, and the
fine vows you made are unfulfilled.

In all things be slow to promise, prompt to per-
form. You can fairly estimate what you would do
with much by what you do with little. If you say
that you now are too poor to share, you will find
other reasons for not sharing when your supply becomes great. Be honest with yourself. You have
gains to make, aside from all hopes of gains in
finances. One of these is integrity. Learn not to
cheat yourself.

Do you pray that you may be prospered in order
that you may give to others? If you do, change your
prayer; pray that others may be prospered. The only
way in which you can duplicate God in the mat-

ter of giving is by giving of what you already have.

In practical ways, you will find that sharing and expectancy are the beginnings of financial increase. The widow did not wait until she had accumulated much meal and oil. She did not pray that she might be prospered to the end that she might be able to care for the prophet. She shared what she had, expecting supply to continue. Then her prosperity began.

Your application of your mental powers may so far have resulted in a state of which you say, "By yielding to the divine order I have been able to receive health, but my finances do not improve. How can I become prospered?" If you will use your mind as intelligently in the matter of supply as you used it in the matter of health, you will find yourself financially prospered as well as healed. The substance that renews your body is the substance that renews your bank account. Your mind transmutes substance. Of gold the government makes coins; of the same metal the smith makes works of art; the jeweler makes personal adornments. Gold, which is an adaptation of substance, adapts itself to demand. The adaptations to which gold lends itself are not many; the adaptations to which substance lends itself are as numerous as your wants are, or as they ever can become. Treat substance as the obliging presence of all that you need, appearing in your body as health, in your affairs as supply. Then, you will become acquainted with your resource and you will find that it will yield to you in all your requirements of it.

THE WEDDING GUESTS: There was a wedding in Cana of Galilee. Substance as wine failed. Substance as water continued. The ruler of the feast was troubled. Embarrassment might ensue. "Water," he may have mused, "comes from God, a free gift bestowed as He will. It pours easily from the clouds and eagerly is received by the earth. It filters through the soil and comes out, a sweet and cleansing flow. Of water there is no lack. But wine is another matter. To garner an abundant harvest of grapes the vineyard must be worked on; the vines and the clusters must be protected and encouraged by the husbandman. Then, there is the wine press, also the rich, ripening juice. Wine comes from nature; it is the reward of working and waiting. I need wine for the guests."

In so arguing the ruler of the feast anticipated your views concerning forms of substance: The free gift of God none may check; it comes when He is gracious enough to bestow. The toil-earned reward fails. God is constant to His purposes. Nature is capricious.

The Guest at the feast spoke to the servants, instructing them in certain matters. The servants refilled the waterpots with water. The empty wine skins, the drained ewers, they touched not. But forthwith they drew from the waterpots that which they bore to the ruler of the feast. Wine it was; good wine, such wine as hosts were wont to serve at the beginning of feasts when drinkers had keenness of taste.

How is water made wine? How is mineral made tree? What grew your body?

The elemental resource is God. Human consciousness objectifies the resource in general as nature, in particular as water, wine. If there were more than one substance each substance would be peculiar in character, and the ruler of the feast would have had to send out for wine. As there is but one substance, that substance is adaptable to meet all your needs. The Guest at the wedding feast knew the adaptability of substance. He co-operated with the adaptable nature of substance, and wine was drawn out where water had been put in.

God has given you Himself as your resource. He does not bestow Himself occasionally; He has given you Himself as your steady, your eternal resource. The toil-earned reward is good, but better is it to let substance come forth, shaped to fit the need before you become aware of the need; then need cannot arise.

The conversion of water into wine occurred at a wedding. Adaptability exists in union, in oneness. Substance is water or it is wine, dependent on your need. As resource, substance is one. In use, substance becomes many.

All the forms of substance that you know are adaptations of the one elemental substance. Each form of substance contains the potentiality of all other forms of substance. The Guest knew this, and by treating the available supply as the desired form of supply, water became wine.

The parable of the marriage feast offers you two more rules having to do with supply. When you observe these rules you will be able to adapt substance to your requirements. The rules are:

1. Consider substance as one, not many.

2. Treat the available form of supply as if it were the required form of supply.

If your understanding of your resource stops at the knowledge that supply will last, you may duplicate the experience of the widow: Your supply will continue, but it will be scanty. This is the hand-to-mouth program from which many find it hard to depart. If to continuation of substance you add adaptability of substance, forms of substance will multiply for you. But continuation and adaptability may not give you abundance; they will produce for you in the forms to which you give your consent. The prophet will have oil and meal; the ruler of the feast will have enough wine for the guests. You are the prophet when you say, "I can hold my job. My wages are small, but they will keep me from starving." You are the ruler of the feast when you say, "I can feed, clothe, and house my family, but I cannot give my children the education that I should like them to have."

In taking stock of your abilities and of your manifest supply, you may say, "There is not enough to go around." Not enough of you, to be sure. But there is enough of God to go around, and since substance is the body of God, there is enough of substance to go around. Your restricted supply is due to your restricted treatment and consideration of substance.

THE BANQUET IN THE DESERT: The Guest at Cana of Galilee had become the Host of the desert.

The guests were expectant of a spiritual feast; this they were given. At the conclusion of that feast the Host offered them food of another kind. The Host was also Teacher; He had taught them, "All things whatsoever the Father hath are mine." He would now in part demonstrate that teaching, that they might learn to demonstrate and so be approved in "He that believeth on me, the works that I do shall he do also."

Advisers of the Host suggested that He send the multitude to those places where food was to be seen as already manifest. Had the Host believed as the widow had believed, that supply would dwindle to the vanishing point; had He believed with the ruler of the feast that substance is fixed in form and non-convertible; had He believed with His apostles that food is to be found in some places and not to be found in other places, He would have dismissed the multitude that each person might shift for himself. But He knew that supply may be made to continue. He knew that substance is convertible to all forms that the mind decrees. In addition to His knowledge of these facts, He knew that no place is barren of the element that nourishes.

Not knowing that substance is everywhere, they said to Him, "Shall we go and buy food for these people? We have money enough to buy a morsel for each." He answered, "Feed them with what you have." Not knowing that substance is exhaustless, they said, "We have but five loaves and two fishes—little fishes, and," with eloquent gesture toward the multitude, "what is this among so many?"

The Host took the supply. He looked to the Source of supply and spoke words of thanks. Then He broke the bread and the fish, passed the pieces to His apostles, who distributed to the throng.

One account relates that when a loaf or a fish was broken it immediately was entire again. The Host never took His hands off the visible supply. Bread and fish passed through His hands in a steady flow, and in the desert where only He could discern supply, He fed the multitude.

You may have been taught that the ability of the Host to feed the multitude from that scanty store was due to His having given thanks. This is good teaching, but it does not cover the vital fact in the situation. Thanking God for supply may be a formal courtesy or it may be the expression of a profound gratitude. In either event it is not sufficient to produce increase. When you know whence comes your supply you instinctively will give thanks.

Substance flows under your hand, an unending stream of potential forms. If you keep your hand on the stream, you can break substance in any form and in any quantity. When you take your hand off the stream of substance you cease to break. Thousands or few, substance is sufficient. Desert or garden, substance abounds. Neither place nor numbers can dismay you when you have rightly related yourself to your resource. Seed time and harvest and the seasons thereof are mental processes slowed to the rhythms of the fictitious world. Immediate response is the harvest of your reliance on the eternal resource.

There must be no waste. All things are for use.

Pick up the fragments. They will remind you that supply is in even the desert. They will compel you to think of the source that flows for you everywhere, all the time. Pick up the fragments; substance is everywhere, but waste is contempt for the resource.

The banquet in the wilderness specifies two more requirements for your perfect co-operation with the law of supply. These requirements are:

1. Look to the Source. Spontaneous thanks will arise from your heart.

2. Keep your hands on the stream of substance. Break according to the need.

If conditions look doubtful, continue to break in the form that you require. If substance seems to dwindle, break opulently. Whatever comes, whatever goes, keep your hands on the stream of substance, and break, break, break in the fashion that satisfies your need. This treatment of substance will make you able to feed any multitude that may assemble in your life.

There is no numbering of the avenues through which supply may come to you. The avenues that you close stay their caravans of richest offerings from remote lands; through them you receive nothing. The avenues that you open will turn their sparkling treasures into the strong room of your consciousness; these treasures are available supply. Of them you may receive as you will. Your resource is as far-reaching as the universe. Here is the concluding lesson on the law of supply:

THE SHEKEL: Taxes were due. There was no money in hand with which to pay. The Son tested

Peter's attitude toward tribute. No protests were made; no growling over taxes complicated the question. Peter could have said, "I will call my brethren; we will fish and sell our catch, that there may be a shekel to pay for thee and me." Or, with a mind to evasion, he might have said, "We are sons, and not strangers. Why pay the tax?"

But the Son would pay the tax, "lest we cause them to stumble," as He tenderly said. So Peter again became a fisherman, but not that he might sell his catch and by so doing come into possession of tribute money for the Son and for himself.

In all other cases of the Son's special handling of substance results are described. The narrative of the fish and the tribute money closes with the words, "take up the fish that first cometh up; and when thou hast opened his mouth, thou shalt find a shekel: that take, and give unto them for me and thee." Why carry the story farther? The tribute was paid. In the course of your development you learn that when the Christ speaks the work is done. Unless you prize superfluities you do not say that a heavy rain fell and soaked the ground. You say that a heavy rain fell. The Son gave instructions; the apostle followed instructions. No prolongation of the account is required.

The incident of the coin in the mouth of the fish has been interpreted to mean that the fish represents increase; that the word of plenty often spoken eventuates in prosperity. The interpretation is good, but not complete.

Another teaching in regard to supply is that you

must not expect it to come to you through any special avenue. This is a good teaching, but it does not meet the whole situation. The important reason for not looking to a special avenue of supply is that, expecting your supply from a given source, your expectation takes on the nature of suggestion. You may suggest to yourself concerning yourself, but you may not suggest to another for any purpose.

The great teaching contained in the tribute money miracle is that you are to expect your supply through all avenues of contact with life. Not from one specified point, not from two or more specified points; but from all points of the universe your good is crowding toward you. If you would coincide in full with the law of supply, you must give it these two final considerations:

1. Supply comes from the expected source in the expected way.

2. Supply comes from unexpected sources, in unexpected ways.

You are the one who is able to shape substance.

Substance is the presence of God. It does not fail.

Substance is adaptable to all my demands. The form that is necessary to my well-being appears.

The stream of substance flows through my hands. I keep my hands on the stream of substance, and break according to my need.

Substance is everywhere. It comes to me from expected and from unexpected sources.

NONRESISTANCE
Chapter 9

You may think of nonresistance as an indifferent, spiritless yielding to whatever occurs. You may think of it as a teaching fit only for the unfit, and as a practice suited only to those who are incapable of self-defense.

If you so think, you wholly miss the meaning of the word and of the act. Nonresistance is stronger than resistance; its practice requires more mind capacity than is required for resistance; its appeal is to the divine thing in you. It is the essence of God.

You may think of resistance as the virility that asserts, attains, and maintains dominance. You may think of it as a teaching that will make you mentally strong, and as a practice that will gain for you the plaudits and the prestige accorded to the powerful.

If you so think, you wholly accord with the ideals of the fictitious world. Resistance is not strength; it is the weakness of ignorance that matches the puny personal against the all-conquering impersonal. Though it prevails for a day, a year, a century; it finally will fail. You, who survive the universes and inhabit eternity, should array yourself on the side of things eternal. You should know that a weak man fights and that a strong man governs himself to higher purposes, that the appeal of resistance is to the beast, that its essence is diabolic.

You may think of resistance as the clash of armed forces; as Titan writhing in the grip of Titan; as the opposing of human devices to the moods of nature; as the bitter wrangling of verbal controversy. All these are forms of resistance. They are indicative of another form of resistance in which they have their beginnings. They are the surface ripples of a mighty current agitated by the friction of swift tide and stony channel.

Resistance means, "To oppose . . . by inertness or active force, physically or mentally."

You mentally resist more than you physically resist. You feel that you so much respect yourself that you would not engage in a fisticuff or in a cheapening quarrel. But for all this fastidiousness in your surface life, you may mentally resist with a fierceness that has on the temper of your life and on the material of your body an effect more demoralizing than that of pugilistic or brawling resistance.

Mental resistance is mental opposition; it is the animus that gives rise to physical and to disputatious oppositions. It is the spirit that steels your mind to rule or to destroy, that sets you as adamant against or for a thing; that diffuses in your consciousness a pugnacity that banishes mental quietude. Mental resistance is the fact and the act in all the resistance that you exercise.

Hurts are produced by resistance. It always takes at least two to make a quarrel. If you resist in any way, you make yourself a candidate for bruises, for buffetings, for postponements.

The things that you meet in life do not hurt you. They are powerless to affect you. But your reaction to them may hurt you. If you resist by active opposition, you most certainly will be hurt. Even though you be acclaimed the victor, you will be scarred by the wounds of the contest. You will be hurt to the measure of the hurt that you would bestow; invariably you will be hoist by your own petard. You built your petard for hoisting purposes. In the relation of reaction to action, the instrument devised for opposition will oppose you. Carrying the teachings to a practical application, you may wish to ask in regard to physical oppositions, "Suppose that I am in unfamiliar territory; it is pitch dark; I run into a stone wall, and am hurt. Why am I hurt?"

The obvious answer to the question is, "The physical opposition of your body to the physical opposition of the stone wall produces the hurt." But there are other oppositions more potent than those. The impact of your body against the wall sets into action a sequence of thoughts, all of which may be resistant. Your mind flares in resentment against the darkness, the strangeness, the complement of circumstances that eventuates in the collision. Also, your instinctive thought is, "The wall is hard. Of course I shall be hurt." Resisting the teachings of nonresistance, you ask, "Am I to dissolve my body, in order that it may not resist the wall? Or should I dissolve the wall, in order that it may not resist my body?"

The nature of your mental reactions on striking the wall causes you to be hurt.

You are capable of developing nonresistance to a degree that will render your flesh impervious to hurt. Thousands of persons know how to be nonresistant to spattering drops of boiling oil, and are unhurt by them. Thousands of persons are practicing the nonresistance that protects them from taking cold on being drenched by chilly rain. Thousands of persons know how to defer hunger and thirst; to have crushed fingers assume normality on release; to hold so calm a poise through nonresistance that the flesh registers no hurt in experiences that produce intense hurt in those who resist.

Out of my own experience with the protective nature of nonresistance, I give you the following:

I was due at an evening entertainment. I had turned off the lights and had reached the door. Then I remembered that my ticket was in a drawer of my desk. Without putting on the lights, I returned to my desk, stooped to open the drawer. I was moving rapidly. My cheek bone came into violent contact with the pointed back of a chair. I saw stars; I saw moons and suns; I saw the whole of the Milky Way.

Instantly I put my hand over my cheek, and said, "Let us see what my faith, coupled to the willingness of God, will do in the matter."

There was no hurting. Ordinarily I would have carried for days the mark of that encounter. There was a slight graining of the skin, but no redness, no bruise, no soreness. Had I made a fist and struck the chair, I should have had a discolored face and a blackened knuckle. As it was, the encounter left no visible reminder.

Should the blow on my face be repeated would the immunity from hurt be repeated? Not unless I again instantly could make myself nonresistant.

Mental resistance is the act of receiving hurt. Mental nonresistance is the act of refusing hurt.

The essence of nonresistance is unity. You are not isolated from the rest of the universe. You are an indispensable part of the universe, and as such the universe loves, protects, and cherishes you. In so caring for you the universe is self-preserving. You are safe. You are inconceivably valuable. Nothing opposes you. You are in the midst of friends.

The practice of nonresistance becomes easy when you take the attitude toward the universe in entirety and toward each entity of the universe in particular that the universe takes toward you. The universe is not isolated from you. It is indispensable to you, and as such, you love, protect, and cherish what it contains. Whatever of altruism distinguishes your attitude in this respect, there is a practical side to the attitude; the practical side is self-preservation.

The universe is safe. It is inconceivably valuable to you. You oppose nothing. You are one of the friendly host that environs all friendly things.

Nonresistance is not the line of least resistance. By following the line of least resistance you may be able temporarily to evade a responsibility. But no responsibility can forever be avoided. If the thing be disagreeable in contemplation, cease to contemplate it; go out to meet it, serenely nonresistant. You will find that your passage through it will be as uneventful as the passage of the Israelites between the walled waters of the sea. The line of least resistance may be the trek of the coward. Nonresistance is the triumphal highway of the hero of the universe—the man that has won consciousness of his identity, his place, his everlastingness.

When you are nonresistant you do not oppose, mentally or physically. You are insured against the friction of resistance. Mental resistance excites your nerves, makes them tense, burns them out; you become irritable, apprehensive. It saps the fluids of your body, and makes your flesh sensitive. Your life takes on two interests: defense of what you call your rights, and defense of your body. Mental resistance challenges to warfare all the phantoms of the fictitious world. Nonresistance cancels all these, and brings you tranquillity in place of perplexity.

Nonresistance means not to oppose, mentally or physically. In nonresistance there is no misuse of power through combativeness or through defensive tactics. The strength of all your gifts can be turned to the creation of harmonies.

Nonresistance is the defense against which no attack can be launched. To the material and to the nonmaterial antagonists bred of resistance, it is as a cloak of light, impenetrable to eyes that see only in darkness. Shielded by the cloak you proceed with your mission. Nonresistance commands omnipotence. The strength of Jesus was in His nonresistant attitude toward God. "I am meek and lowly in heart," He said, not in any way opposing the only power that He recognized. He avowed that He was not doing the will of man, but that He was manifesting the will of Omnipotence as testimony of Omnipotence in the realm of impotence. "They crucified Him, therefore so much for non-

resistance," do you say? Those who tried to oppose
Him could do no more than oppose their own ideas
of Him. They could not find Him; they never so
much as looked upon Him. He was hidden in the
dazzling cloak of light that their eyes could not
penetrate. Borne by the wings of Omnipotence,
swathed in the light of heaven, He proceeded toward
His objective. Had He resisted there still would
have been Golgotha, but there would have been no
Easter morning in the garden of Joseph.

In any warfare in which you find yourself engaged you are the one who wars and the one who is
warred against. You war against your own thoughts
of nature, of people, of life. The universe is at
peace. Your skirmishes are on the surface; they do
not reach into the heart of life. If you think that
you hate others you hate merely what your imperfect
vision claims to see in others. If you distrust others,
your distrust is proof that you doubt the integrity
of the universe. If you resist anything, you but resist the opinion that you have formed in relation to
that thing.

Only sophistry or ignorance would argue that
the teaching here given incites to acts banned by
the law. Nonresistance fulfills the law of the universe. When you co-operate with the law of the
universe, you easily and naturally keep step with
the law in all realms of your experience. You obey
without wrangling; your understanding of the laws
that operate in the real world gives you patience, and
even sympathy, with whatever tentative measures
may be adopted by worlds not wholly real. Living in

the consciousness that your interests and the interests of the universe are identical, adjustment precedes every act. Nonresistance preserves and prospers you.

You resist whatever you oppose, criticize, or resent. When you begin to practice nonresistance you find that you have been resisting in more ways than you would have enumerated. You find inconsistencies, contradictions. You learn that nonresistance applies where you would not have it apply, quite as thoroughly as it does where you would have it apply. Perhaps you are one of that large number who aver that they worship God in nature. If you worship God in nature, you worship Him in barren waste and in pestilential fen, as truly as you worship Him in majestic forest and in sunny meadow. If you worship God in nature, your vision penetrates the fictitious and discerns the real.

If you worship God in nature, you worship Him in weather, in cold that numbs your flesh and in desert blast that drives the stinging sand against your parched cheek; in prolonged rains, in droughts that sear the landscape, in lashing blizzards that obscure your path and push you into unknown regions, in hurricanes on land and on sea. If you resist, resent, grumblingly flinch before any of these, you do not worship God in nature. Nonresistance renders you impervious to the moods and to the inclemencies of weather. The Psalmist, knowing the value of nonresistance in a land semitropical, said, "The sun shall not smite thee."

If you have been ill for a long time, you resent the pain, the feebleness, the seclusion imposed. You

begin to recover; everyone is delighted; your friends
felicitate you. Improvement continues; matters begin to move in normal routine. The tender atten-
tions, the solicitous inquiries concerning your state,
cease. You miss the deferences that you have been
receiving; your memory is not yet cleared of your
recent experiences, and you feel that after all you
are not so well as people think you are. There are oc-
casional recurrences of former symptoms, former
sufferings. But your friends do not regard them se-
riously; they know that you are recovering. You feel
that the world is callous; you are hurt, piqued. You
resist returning health because it quenches the spot-
light that has been playing on you. The state of your
feeling is that of the woman whom a friend of mine
tried to encourage:

The woman had been ill. She had recovered
sufficiently to appear on the street. Meeting her, my
friend said,

"Why, you're well again! How splendid!"

The woman said, "No; I'm not well."

My friend was puzzled, but hoping to make an
encouraging suggestion, spoke of the change in
the woman's appearance: "But you certainly are
looking well."

And the woman who a short time previously
had been confined to her home with illness, but
who was now abroad attending to shopping con-
cerns, answered peevishly, "I don't care how I look;
I guess I know how I feel."

If you consider yourself poor and if you also
resist the poverty that you have brought into your

life, you will have double work in winning your supply: You will have to dismiss the consciousness of
poverty and you will have to become nonresistant to
supply. So long as you treat poverty as an unavoidable experience, poverty will thrust its gaunt form
before your eyes and will snivel in rags by your
side. If you ask how you can become nonresistant
to supply, the answer is:

Supply is a part of the universe; you are a part
of the universe. The unity that prevails in the universe makes you and supply to be one.

If you criticize the religious faith of anyone, you
resist his faith. Resistance to religion in any form
makes you nonreligious. Religion binds; it does not
separate. In every religion there are points that you
can accept; the accepted points bind you to every
individual who believes the religion in its entirety.
The monist believes that one principle works in the
universe; the deist believes that God exists; the
Christian believes that God is and that He manifests as Christ. In generalization an essential unity
appears in the three, but nonessential separateness
of detail has been emphasized. Through emphasis of
detail absence of unity seems apparent. Resistance
centers on detail; nonresistance accepts the generalization. If you agree where you can agree and refrain from considerations of points that you do not
accept, you keep unity with the universe. Agreement
is feasible when your mind seeks agreement. That
truth was first brought to my mind in the incident
which I here relate:

The prayer meeting was open for expression of

faith on the part of the laity. Consequently I spoke.

After I had concluded a man in the congregation arose. He said that he indorsed everything that Miss Shanklin had said. Then he proceeded to review particular statements on which he said he agreed. If I understood what he meant he had not understood what I meant. But he said that he agreed with me. Mentally I said, "Good; I don't know what he means in those particulars in which he says he agrees with me, but if he is willing to agree, we will agree."

At the conclusion of this talk a woman arose. She said that she wished to express her approval of all the matters wherein Mr. Blank had supported what Miss Shanklin had said. Then she proceeded to review the points which she indorsed. If I understood what she meant and if I understood what Mr. Blank meant, this woman had not understood what either Mr. Blank or I had said. But she said that she agreed with us, and this statement I considered a sufficient basis of unity. Mentally I said, "Good, again. If the two of them understand me I do not understand either of them. But they say that they agree with me. So we will agree, whether we agree or not."

Always there is ground for agreement. If you do not find that ground, grant its presence; agree or withdraw in peace. Resistance will fret you, throw you out of correspondence with your association. When you are nonresistant your associations are frictionless, and your growth is unaccompanied by pain.

Nonresistance is not mere tolerance. It includes none of the assumed superiorities of the personal mind. It is a positiveness that offers no opposition, that does not take account of opposition. Being non-resistant, you do not feel yourself of higher grade than others. You do not consider differences; you consider likenesses. You have no enemies, because you are not an enemy. You do not war with nature, and nature is peaceful toward you. The energies of your body are adjusted to opportunities. You feel the glow of heaven's lasting summer within the frost that tingles your flesh, the coolness of mountain airs within the sirocco's breath. You can run without being hurried. You can perspire without being hot. You rest, not because you are exhausted, but because you would have released in you the reservoirs of that strength to which nonresistance holds the key. You can surrender and be victor.

If by "having insomnia" you have been resisting the repose that should come at night, you can through nonresistance make the wakeful hours a trysting season with your Lord; peace and the needed sleep will come. If by "working too hard" you have been resisting your work, you can by nonresistantly waiting on your Lord make His capability your capability; then work and strength will be brought to a parity. If by trying to string too many beads on the thread of time you have become resistant to the limi-tation of days, you can by nonresistance work in the amplitude of eternity.

Nonresistance is ownership. What you love and enjoy is yours, regardless of what titles are held, regardless of who holds the titles. If you resist the fact that the thing is not yours as a matter of manifest possession, you deny the essence of the thing.

When you do not resist what you call your mental limitations, the boundaries of your consciousness expand, and the veiled intelligence discloses itself.

If you are nonresistant toward years the passing of the years will not age you. You continue, but you do not grow old. Your life is transferred from time to eternity. Death is not hailed as the crown of life nor dreaded as the punishment for sin. It ceases to have a place in your mind. States of consciousness come, are succeeded by other states, but you do not die; you continue to live.

When you are nonresistant toward your good, your good runs to meet you. I have found that I never win until I become willing to do without the trophy. I have learned to say to whatever seems worth having, "If you do not want me as much as I want you, I do not want you at all. I can do without you, and sorrow not; but I will welcome you if you come. Take your choice. It does not matter to me."

This declaration or any declaration of similar spirit must be wholly sincere, or confusion and disappointment will follow its use. Sincerely avowed, what is worth while responds; what is not worth while fades from consciousness.

Do not let yourself become so important to yourself that you come to consider yourself the guardian of the morals and the rights of the race. You are to work with all law, but do not be agitated for the sanctity of any law. You know that the spiritual law never is defeated; it operates regardless of your approval or disapproval; therefore, you do not have to invoke its action in any case. You know that the social law automatically penalizes or rewards; you do not have to set it into motion. You know that the civil law has ample machinery for the enforcement of its mandates; you need not be exercised for its survival or for its effectiveness. If you are at all wise, you will keep yourself clear of the bigotry that rejoices in punishments or that decrees punishments. Emotional resistance to illegal acts is a merciless weapon that the law of mind will turn against you. "Neither do I condemn thee," said purity to impurity. By that sweet act of nonresistance was revived the drugged virtue of the sinner, who then forsook sin.

Do not flatter yourself into thinking that people persecute you because of your superiority. You will not be persecuted if you do not accept persecution. The fact of persecution may be wholly within yourself, a reaction that indicates how you feel toward one whom you acknowledge as your superior. Few criticisms will be made of your faith if you really know your faith and consistently live it. The world is little interested in what you believe. It is tremendously interested in what your belief causes you to do.

Do not resist persons' opinions of you; do not form opinions of persons that will cause them to resist. If you refrain in these respects, peace will flow from you and to you. Your responsibility begins and ends with yourself. The coming act will be your choice; with it you have all to do. The act that was is with God; with it you have nothing to do. Say to naughty Nero, smirking under the red night skies, "Go on with your bonfires, but don't expect me to stay awake to look at them. I've work to do tomorrow and I need my sleep."

Do not resist your experiences by being ashamed when you have not known how to let God deliver you. When you say of any matter, "I have not yet demonstrated," the reason for the delay is apparent to one who knows the source of demonstration. The demonstrator demonstrates himself. When "I" demonstrates, it demonstrates itself; that self is the personal; it federates with time and time involves postponements. Do not oppose God by trying to demonstrate yourself. Then God will demonstrate Himself; His demonstration will be of the nature of a miracle in your life.

Do not resist ridicule of your confidence. One who does not accept, "with God all things are possible," resists Omnipotence. Do not resist that one's resistance. God does not need your defense. Your defense of yourself weakens you by disintegrating your moral structure. One, speaking from the *who* consciousness, may ask you,

"So you really believe that nothing is impossible with God?"

Speaking from the *what* consciousness, you answer,

"Yes."

The questioner then thinks that he has you in a corner. He asks,

"Can God make a two-year-old tree in a minute of time?"

Your answer is, "Yes; and He can do even better than that. God does not work with time, but with eternity, where His works have been completed from the beginning. God's two-year-old tree already is made; always has been made; but with your present focus on life it will take you two years to see it."

Considering resistance in the sense of opposition by inertness, you will see that there are instances when resistance has virtually the meaning of non-resistance. This use is rare; it is employed to indicate dismissal from mind and nonrecognition in action. In nearly all cases, resistance means to oppose by physical or by mental force. The exceptional use serves the valuable purpose of reconciling two New Testament statements that otherwise appear contradictory. Jesus taught, "Resist not him that is evil." The meaning is, do not oppose by active force anyone or any thing at any time. If you oppose, there will be a reaction as opposition; there will be war. James taught, "Resist the devil, and he will flee from you." The meaning is ignore evil and it will not attack you; it will retreat from your presence until it becomes lost to you. This use of resistance is equivalent to the denial that is taught by metaphysicians.

Nonresistance will protect you from all the assaults that can be attempted by the inhabitants of the fictitious world. It will open for you an entrance to the world of vital potentialities, the living soul and God. If at times it seems that the phantoms of

the fictitious press close, shut your eyes to them
and call to the shining presences of the real world.
When you again open your eyes, you will see that
you are encompassed by the hosts of heaven. If along
the way to your objective the floods pour their strong
tides against you, stand still for a time; set your
mind in prayer and let the currents flow. They will
drain by. You will not have been delayed.

The heart of the test is this: Can you hold yourself levelly nonresistant toward apparent injustice
directed toward you?

The unjust act ceases to be unjust when you accept it by resisting. If you do not resist, the act is
not unjust to you, because you do not receive it. The
act then belongs wholly to the actor. Let him dis-
pose of it as he will. To him, only, his intent is real,
and you can afford calmly to ignore the entire proceeding. As you value your peace of mind, your
progress, never let yourself be hurt by what anyone
does.

Do not let yourself consider retribution, to be
administered by yourself or by the law. Do not betray yourself by the reproach, "I thought that he
was my friend; but he is not, for he has failed me."
If you chose blindly, the failure that you proclaim is
not in the one you chose, but in you. If you have
felt that you were misrepresented, know this: The
lie never gets beyond the lips of the liar, until you
attract it to yourself by opposing it. Regard the event
as remote in time and space; look on it as purposeless, impotent, if you are not strong enough to keep
your eyes away from it entirely. Dismiss the im-

passionate personal; let it wait at the horizon of consciousness. Let the dispassionate impersonal take charge, and the event will become for you as if it never had occurred. You will see that you were not hurt; you will learn that resistance is a labor that brings you no gain. Because God is unoffending and unoffended He also is nonresistant. When you become nonresistant no stain can be painted on you; no hurt can find shelter in you.

Pray, "Thy kingdom come." In so praying you ask that the nonresistance of God become your protection. Your prayer will be granted. You will cease to resist. The peace of the kingdom will be yours.

Pray, "Thy will be done." In so praying you ask the nonresistance of God to motivate you. Your prayer will be granted. Nonresistance will give you easy access to the shrine of your objective. "It is finished."

God the nonresistant, also is God the irresistible. Nonresistance is the irresistibility that without hurt delivers you whenever there is need of deliverance; that wraps you in the shining mantle of God's protecting love; that flings wide for you the portals of the highest heaven; that within the tempest's chant sings the conqueror's anthem. It is the bud on the tree of life that tells of fruits to follow. It is the coolness of crystal waters, without which your soul would grievously thirst. It is the day star of a fairer era in your eternity. It is God living you in holiest manifestation.

You are heaven's nonresistant, all-conquering **hero.**

*The universe loves, protects, and cherishes me.
I am nonresistant to all things in the universe.
Thine, O God, is the kingdom, Thine the power,
Thine the glory, through newborn eternities in end-
less processional. Amen.*

ABOUT THE AUTHOR

Imelda Octavia Shanklin was born on October 1, 1865, in Waubeek, Iowa, to a predominantly Methodist family and was probably influenced by the Quakers who were prominent in the area. She never married and, prior to coming to Unity, taught school and wrote, for a time, on historical and political subjects.

In 1909 Imelda Shanklin began working for Silent Unity. At that time Unity School of Christianity had a working staff of four people, including Imelda. Unity cofounder Myrtle Fillmore served as editor of *Wee Wisdom*® magazine and Imelda wrote articles that were published in it. On September 8, 1918, Unity cofounder Charles Fillmore ordained her as a Unity minister. Also in 1918 she was named editor of *Wee Wisdom*® and then in 1925, editor in chief of all Unity publications.

During her editorship, *Wee Wisdom*® expanded its circulation to all foreign countries where English was spoken. She wrote for all of Unity's periodicals including *Unity Magazine, Weekly Unity, New, Progress, Youth, Good Business,* and, of course, *Wee Wisdom*®. In 1930 she resigned her position and moved to Viola, Iowa, in order to devote her life to writing along metaphysical lines.

In addition to her writing, Imelda taught Sunday school at the local Methodist church and was active in the Unity work in Cedar Rapids, Iowa. She is most famous for her book *What Are You?* which

161

came out in 1929. Other books she wrote include *Selected Studies,* later called *All Things Made New,* which originally came out in 1921, *Lessons for Young Students* in 1924, and *Treasure Box* in 1927—none of which are currently in print. She also self-published a book for young metaphysicians called *Our Enchanted Island* in 1940 and wrote another book that has since been lost. Imelda made her transition on June 12, 1953, in Viola.

Imelda Shanklin is remembered, and her writings reprinted, because she communicated a spiritual power that came directly from her personal relationship with God. She still speaks to students of Truth because she provides answers to questions she herself had to answer.

Printed in the U.S.A.   B0008-13527-2C-8-07 LS

Printed in the United States
207144BV00002B/175-396/A